Hallucination-focused Therapy

Hallucination-focused Integrative Treatment (HIT) is a specific treatment for auditory verbal hallucinations which integrates techniques from CBT, systems therapy, psychoeducation, coping training, rehabilitation and medication. It emphasizes active family involvement, crisis intervention when required and specialized motivational strategies. In clinical trials HIT has been proven to have long lasting and wider ranging effects than other therapies, high patient satisfaction scores and a low drop-out rate.

In *Hallucination-focused Integrative Therapy*, Jack Jenner presents a full manual for using HIT with patients. Divided into five parts, the book offers a clear and straightforward explanation of each aspect of the treatment. Part 1 introduces auditory verbal hallucinations in their social and historical context. Part 2 explains the need for an integrative approach to treating them and sets out the 11-step diagnostic procedure. Part 3 describes the treatment in full, including motivational strategies, the constituent modules and how to integrate them, flexible implementation of a tailor-made procedure and its overall effectiveness. It also demonstrates the use of HIT with specific patient groups, including those suffering from trauma, children and adolescents, those who are suicidal and those with learning difficulties. Part 4 examines other hallucination-focused therapies. Finally, Part 5 covers insight-oriented psychotherapies. The book also includes several appendices of supplementary material which enhance the content.

Illustrated throughout with case studies and clinical material, *Hallucination-focused Integrative Therapy* will be of interest to psychiatrists, psychologists, neurologists, psychiatric nurses and social workers working with patients who experience auditory verbal hallucinations.

Jack A. Jenner is a consultant psychiatrist and psychotherapist registered for children and adolescents as well as adults in the Netherlands. He has been presenting and giving workshops internationally on issues relating to emergency psychiatry, suicidology, psychiatry and hallucinations for over 30 years. He is the director of AUDITO, a centre for diagnosis and treatment of people with auditory verbal hallucinations, and is the creator of HIT. He has formerly been associate professor of community psychiatry at Groningen University and visiting professor at Banaras Hindu University.

'In this book you will find a novel treatment for persons who suffer from voice-hearing. Over the last 25 years Dr. Jenner has developed and researched a concise goal-directed and evidence-based treatment: HIT! This book is a must read for those interested in treating persons who very often suffer for long periods, despite biological treatments, from voice-hearing. You will find in this book a systematic approach, with many clinical details and which pays special attention to treating specific subgroups of patients, e.g. children. We are very happy that his work on HIT is now also available for a large international audience.' – **Bert L.B. Luteijn MD, Psychiatrist and Chair of the Dutch HIT Implementation Network, the Netherlands**

'A brilliant book that places "hands-on" therapeutic interventions in an innovative theoretical framework. Jenner's pioneering treatment for auditory verbal hallucinations is acceptable to patients and relatives. There is a spirit of personal involvement and a willingness to go beyond guidelines towards personal needs, written in a coherent style. Exquisite case-vignettes illustrate the "what" and the "how" of his method across a range of contexts and patient needs including suicidality, treatment-resistant schizophrenia, borderline personality disorder, post-traumatic stress disorder, intellectual disability and childhood psychosis. This book will keep us going for years.' – **Jim van Os, Professor of Psychiatry, Maastricht University Medical Centre, the Netherlands**

'In this outstanding resource, Jack Jenner provides an elegant and helpful synthesis of the HIT program. Evidence-based strategies to relieve distressing hallucinations are presented in depth, always illustrated with key clinical cases. An absolute must-read book for every clinician working with hallucinations.' – **Renaud Jardri, University of Lille, France**

'This book compiles the long experience of one of the leading experts in the therapeutic approach to hallucinations. Jack Jenner has developed the most complete program currently existing on hallucination-focused integrative therapy, with a wide range of very practical modules of sequenced and combined interventions, which may be adapted to the specific needs, characteristics and circumstances of each patient and his/her hallucinatory experiences. Learning and conducting this hallucination-focused integrative therapy is of great interest for all mental health professionals working in this field.' – **Manuel González de Chávez, Ex-President of the International Society for Psychological and Social Approaches to Psychosis**

Hallucination-focused Integrative Therapy

A specific treatment that hits auditory verbal hallucinations

Jack A. Jenner

Routledge
Taylor & Francis Group

LONDON AND NEW YORK

First published 2016
by Routledge
2 Park Square, Milton Park, Abingdon, Oxon, OX14 4RN

and by Routledge
711 Third Avenue, New York, NY 10017

Routledge is an imprint of the Taylor & Francis Group, an informa business

British Library Cataloguing in Publication Data
A catalogue record for this book is available from the British Library

Library of Congress Cataloging in Publication Data
Jenner, J. A. (Jacobus Adrianus), 1944-
Hallucination-focused integrative therapy : a specific treatment that hits auditory verbal hallucinations / Jack A. Jenner.
pages cm
Includes bibliographical references and index.
1. Auditory hallucinations—Treatment. I. Title.
RC553.A84J46 2016
616.89—dc23
2015020699

ISBN: 978-1-138-93230-2 (hbk)
ISBN: 978-1-138-93231-9 (pbk)
ISBN: 978-1-315-67935-8 (ebk)

Typeset in Times
by Swales & Willis Ltd, Exeter, Devon, UK
Printed and bound in Great Britain by
Ashford Colour Press Ltd, Gosport, Hampshire

For Marianne
my muse,
beloved love
and companion

Contents

Foreword

Rules and regulations, group-based guidelines and cumbersome classification systems have become so dominant that they may interfere with the therapeutic relationship that is the core ingredient of psychiatric services.

However, defensive reactions are not compatible with innovation and integration of clinical methods. Jenner, therefore, has rendered patients, relatives and the clinical community a service with this positively framed book. His experience in community psychiatry, crisis intervention, psychotherapy, cultural psychiatry and spirituality have been integrated into a treatment for auditory verbal hallucinations (AVHs) that is effective, well appreciated by patients and relatives – and affordable too. His experience, nicely embedded in an innovative theoretical framework, is illustrated across a variety of case vignettes written in a clear and frequently exciting style. I very much like this type of book: strong personal involvement and a coherent message.

Jenner's pioneering work in the area of psychosis has resulted in an open dialogue between the elements of motivational strategy, strong resource group involvement, flexibility of choice within a rich array of modules, 'hands-on' interventions and a search for synergy of pharmacological and psychosocial interventions. His approach is refreshingly innovative, taking elements of the psychotic narrative in a therapeutic reframing exercise that leave the patient feeling more empowered. For example, he challenges a person who is rejecting her medication to use the bitter taste of the medication to ward off hallucinated black birds that pick her flesh. Weird – perhaps. But not when you read it in the context of personalized treatment. No wonder that HIT (Hallucination-focused Integrative Treatment) has a low drop-out and non-compliance rate (9% in patients with a diagnosis of chronic schizophrenia).

I welcome the attention given to special groups such as children, traumatized individuals, the intellectually disabled and other groups.

This book will keep us going for years.

Jim van Os
Professor of Psychiatry
Maastricht University Medical Centre
The Netherlands

Part 1

Auditory verbal hallucinations in context

Chapter 1

Introduction

The focus of this book is on auditory verbal hallucinations (AVHs). Hallucinations are defined as sensory perceptions in the absence of external stimuli. According to the *Diagnostic and Statistical Manual of Mental Disorders* (DSM-IV-TR; American Psychiatric Association, 1994), AVHs are experienced as known or unknown voices that differ qualitatively from one's own thoughts. At present, current definitions of hallucination differ from each other on certain details. This complicates diagnosis and impedes progress in research. The *APA Dictionary of Psychology* (Vanden Bos, 2007) defines hallucination as 'a false sensory perception that has the compelling sense of reality despite the absence of an external stimulus'. This definition is satisfactory in daily practice, but one may question whether it is complete.

Most definitions agree that hallucinations require certain characteristics:

- *Sensory perception.* This discriminates hallucination from imagination, which is a kind of as-if perception lacking the sensory quality of hallucinations.
- *A compelling sense of reality.* This also distinguishes AVHs from imagination (Slade and Bentall, 1988).
- *Uncontrollability.* Slade and Bentall (1988) argue that hallucinations are beyond control. However, while it is true that many hallucinating subjects complain of having no control at all, some certainly have. For example, quite a few voice hearers, especially those with religious themes, are able to evoke their voices. Most voice hearers have at least some control, although this is insufficient in most patients (Jenner, 2012a, 2012b). Some patients have intuitive abilities to regulate their voices, and some therapies report increased mastery of voices following coping training, although patients may still perceive voices. It seems unrealistic not to call these perceptions hallucinations just because they are in some sense controllable.
- *Absence of an external stimulus.* No consensus exists on whether AVHs need to come from the outside world (true hallucination) or from inside the head (pseudohallucination). Voice hearers report variably (i.e. perceiving their voices as coming from outside, inside, and both outside and inside the head). Many tactile hallucinations are experienced within the body. Also, hallucinations may be triggered by external stimuli, such as background noise. These reports raise doubt about the mandatory absence of an external stimulus.

Hallucinations occur in full consciousness. Isolated perceptions, such as hearing one's name, are not pathognomonic for a psychotic disorder. Recent studies have demonstrated the existence of non-psychotic hallucinations as well as hallucinations in the absence of any psychiatric disorder. Some problems remain for the above-mentioned definition of hallucinations. If our perceptions, including hallucinations, are encoded as internal representations, can they be considered 'stimuli'? If not, is adjustment of the definition needed? Are hallucinations ruled out when perceptions are found to be caused by an irregular release of neurotransmitters? Based on a literature review, Van der Zwaard and Polak (1999) argued that the validity of the previously considered definition is weak. They hypothesize a continuum of overlapping categories, including perceptual disorders, flashbacks, dissociative impressions and normal thought and memory processes.

Hallucinations are intriguing phenomena that some individuals welcome for their enlightenment. However, for quite a number of people, hallucinations are highly burdensome and frightening. Fortunately, recent research has shed new light on the phenomena, and promising therapies have been developed. Nevertheless, much has yet to be decided: the current theories of hallucination have important discrepancies, experts are still debating whether hallucinations are pathological phenomena or not, and evidence-based interventions are not widely disseminated. At present the emphasis is largely on psychopathology rather than on significance, spirituality or paranormality. There is still debate as to whether hallucinations are (a) evidence of pathology, (b) symptoms of diseases, (c) normal phenomena, or (d) an expression of paranormal talent. At present, the answer is equivocal. It is clear that a hallucination in itself is not a sufficient condition for mental disorder. The prevalence rate of psychotic symptoms is about 10 times higher than that of properly diagnosed psychotic disorders (van Os et al., 2009). It is not even the nature of hallucinations that primarily determine whether they are socially accepted or labelled pathological, but rather ancillary aspects such as their impact on the person's functioning. Cultural context is pivotal here.

Hypnosis, meditation, psychoactive drugs or medication may all evoke hallucinations. However, they are much more common in certain psychiatric disorders. Disturbed reality testing and misperception are correlated and may lead to hallucinations. Ego functions and cognitive structures can fail to differentiate between reality and fantasy and blur the boundaries between the internal and external world.

Understanding hallucinations, especially bizarre ones, can be difficult for lay people. Literature and films commonly (and falsely) suggest that hallucinations are identical to psychosis and disturbed reality testing. They exaggerate strange, dangerous and bizarre characteristics of some hallucinations. This misrepresentation can easily induce two errors: (1) a rationalization for marginalizing subjects with aberrant perceptions and thoughts, (2) a denial of psychiatric disorders resulting in withheld treatment.

Are hallucinations abnormal?

The prevalence of hallucinations in healthy subjects without somatic and psychiatric disorders is sufficiently high to assume hallucinations to be within the range of normal (psychological) phenomena. This certainly applies to AVHs. Several studies have demonstrated that hallucinations can be induced in healthy subjects by combining suggestions addressed at sensory perception with ambiguous stimuli. Pivotal in this process is the pattern of expectations subjects have. Subjects who have the ability to hallucinate appear to be more sensitive for suggestion than psychiatric patients and healthy non-hallucinating subjects (Haddock *et al.*, 1995; Young *et al.*, 1987). Hallucinatory experiences are far from pathognomonic for specific diseases. For example, according to the DSM-IV-TR hypnagogic and hypnopompic hallucinations at dawn and dusk are normal short-lived phenomena, seldom accompanied by complications. Most subjects begin hallucinating due to the presence of extreme physiological or psychic circumstances, such as sleep deprivation, lengthy solitude (e.g. solo sailors), oxygen deficiency (e.g. mountaineers), extreme situations such as traumatic experiences (e.g. incest and other forms of sexual abuse), robbery, effects of war, imprisonment and torture. Hallucinations and illusions are also common following the loss of a loved one. In one report 82% of elderly subjects were found to experience hallucinations for months after bereavement (Grimby, 1993).

By definition, patients with a diagnosis of schizophrenia hallucinate while fully conscious. However, consciousness may be decreased, as is the case in dissociative trance disorders. Drugs may induce a state of broadened consciousness. The lifetime prevalence rate for AVHs is highest in subjects with dissociative disorders (85%), schizophrenia spectrum disorders (60–70%), psychotic depression (30%), bipolar disorder (47%), post-traumatic stress disorder (PTSD) (30%) and borderline personality disorder (30%) (Hammersley *et al.*, 2003; Landmark *et al.*, 1990; Sidgewick *et al.*, 1894; Tien, 1991; Yee *et al.*, 2005). AVH prevalence among patients with Lewy body dementia is 45%, while they are rare in patients with Alzheimer disease (McKeith *et al.*, 2005).

Important indicators of psychopathological AVHs are failing control, and negative consequences for self-image, self-care, daily activities, social contact and work. Romme and Escher (1989) found that Schneiderian criteria such as the perceived location of AVHs (inside or outside the ear) insufficiently discriminate voice hearers with a psychiatric disorder from those without. The conviction of being able to control the voices was the strongest discriminator.

Hallucinations are not pathognomonic for any particular disorder as they are caused by a wide range of somatic disorders, medications and physiological conditions (Asaad and Shapiro, 1986). Neither do AVH by themselves provide sufficient evidence of an underlying psychiatric disorder, as can be shown by a number of considerations. First, the incidence of AVHs in the general population is far greater than the incidence of psychotic disorders (Rössler *et al.*, 2007; van Os *et al.*, 2000). One large study of persons with hallucinations found that no psychiatric disorder could be established in approximately half of the sample (Tien, 1991). Hallucinations are common among children, with about 9% of 7- and 8-year-olds reporting AVHs. However, only a minority of children with AVHs report these as resulting in suffering or interfering with thinking and daily activities that characterize psychiatric illnesses. Parents gave the majority of these children Child Behavior Checklist (CBCL) scores below the psychopathology cut-off score (Bartels-Velthuis et al., 2010).

Second, hypnagogic and hypnopompic AVHs are normal phenomena according to the DSM-IV-TR.

Third, hearing one's name in the absence of an external stimulus is not a psychotic sign. More than 60% of American college students hear a voice calling their name in the absence of an external stimulus at least once a year (Barrett and Etheridge, 1992). It is unlikely that all of them were psychotic at that time.

Fourth, hallucinations may be caused by a wide range of somatic disorders, such as epilepsy, Charles Bonnet syndrome, deafness, vitamin deficiencies, immunodeficiencies, tumours, infectious disorders with fevers, dehydration and metabolic disorders (Asaad and Shapiro, 1986). A correlation has been found between secondary deafness, paranoia and AVHs. These hallucinations are mainly heard in the deaf ear. Deafness and cerebral disorders often cause musical hallucinations in non-psychotic patients (Almeida et al., 1993; Berrios, 1990).

Fifth, many religions, including Christianity, Sufism, Shamanism and Animism occasionally attribute special abilities, gifts and strength to hallucinating subjects. Their hallucinations are interpreted as supernatural or divine perceptions. Voice hearers' social standing can be ambiguous: sometimes they are held in high regard by their communities on the one hand, and on the other seen as awkward outsiders. In some communities, their status is risky. For example, rain dancers who fail to initiate rain have been known to be killed.

Sixth, consider also the neuroimaging studies that have demonstrated how hallucinations occur simultaneously with increased neuronal firing in sensory-related brain areas. Broca and Wernicke's areas have been shown to be especially active in AVHs (David, 1999; Stephane et al., 2001; Weiss and Heckers, 1999) and visual cortex neurons in visual hallucinations. In other words, the disturbance seems to be more related to interpretation of stimuli than to perception itself.

Romme and Escher (1999) found neither voice hearing itself, nor the Schneiderian criterion third-person hallucinations discriminative between diseased and healthy persons. Instead, it was largely the attribution of negative power to voices and a perceived lack of control and mastery that discriminated between voice hearers with and without a psychiatric disorder. Also, loss of autonomy was an important discriminating factor. Other studies did not find significant associations between psychotic disorders and third-person voices either (Copolov et al., 2004). The ability to control AVHs appeared to be a strong parameter for discriminating psychiatric patients from non-patients (Bartels-Velthuis et al., 2010; Copolov et al., 2004; Honig et al., 1998; Romme and Escher, 1989).

Hallucinations may occasionally have *protective* effects. Jenner et al. (2008) found that over 50% of schizophrenic patients with AVHs reported positive voices and about 40% useful voices that supported them and even were helpful in fulfilling daily activities. Although positive and useful voices are fairly common, the great majority of voice hearers with a psychiatric disorder suffer from rather persistent AVHs with negative content (Jenner *et al.*, 2008). Over 75% of Intervoice members reported the experience of positive voices (Rutten *et al.*, 2007). Fear that treatment will make these helpful voices disappear may be one reason for non-compliance in a substantial number of patients.

The impact of auditory verbal hallucinations

This question about the impact of AVHs may be subdivided into four smaller ones: What impact do AVHs have on voice hearers? In what way do voice hearers interact with their AVHs? What is the meaning of interpersonal relationships, role-expectations, and role-behaviour? Can the personal significance of AVHs be used in therapy?

In a large study of ethnic minorities across England and Wales two-thirds of subjects were not bothered by their AVHs (Tien, 1991). Nevertheless, hallucinations bring about emotions. Reports on the emotional impact of voices suggest a great diversity of responses. Involuntary hallucinations are likely to be more emotionally salient than voluntary hallucinations. Most patients hear their voices frequently and over long periods of time. Almost half of them hear them for over an hour a day. About three-quarters report that the volume is comparable to the loudness of normal conversation. Tien (1991) and Nayani and David (1996) found that about half of the voice hearers studied experienced their AVHs as disturbing or frightening or reported that they made them feel sad, while anger was relatively infrequent. In contrast, AVHs often have a positive meaning too: they may be useful, supportive, pleasant and desired. Between a quarter and three-quarters of voice hearers report experiencing positive voices (Jenner *et al.*, 2008; Sanjuan *et al.*, 2004). About 40% report hearing useful voices that give advice or remind them of plans (Jenner *et al.*, 2008).

Note that 'useful' is not equivalent to 'pleasant' or positive. For example, some of my patients got annoyed at voices that reminded them to take medication. They wanted to get rid of these voices, despite knowing that without their help they risked civil commitment (Jenner, 2013). Stephane *et al.* (2003) found that the degree to which voice hearers ascribe their voices to themselves was related to the degree to which they could control them. Voice hearers who ascribe voices to themselves also put more effort into mastering their voices than voice hearers who attribute these externally.

The relationship between voice hearers and their AVHs is strongly dependent on their particular interpretations and attributions. These are coloured by their personal experiences, conception of humankind, personal worldview, and spirituality. Their reactions to AVHs and their coping repertoire will depend on their psychiatric diagnosis as well as on their relationship to these voices. It is important to know whether their relationship with their voices is in the stage of confusion, organization or stabilization (Romme *et al.*, 1992; see below), as well as the person's orientation towards their voices in the dimensions of love versus hate, one-sided versus interpersonal focus, and identification with the voices versus differentiation. These last three dimensions are strongly related to the emotional loading of the voices, as discussed further throughout the book. Hostile and accusing voices elicit fighting or protest. Subjects tend to surrender to controlling voices, while subjects who feel in control more frequently report a submissive quality to their voices. Patients with borderline personality disorder and those with depression with psychotic features usually have a hostile relationship with their voices. Patients with bipolar disorder tend to have friendlier AVHs. Patients with undifferentiated schizophrenia and psychotic depression usually experience AVHs as friendly when they evoke them, and hostile when it is the voices that initiate the contact. Borderline patients, in contrast, tend to view their voices as hostile irrespective of who took the initiative. Violent patients with schizophrenia hear significantly greater negative tone and content from their AVHs, irrespective of the voices' characteristics: frequency, duration, volume and apparent reality (Benjamin, 1989). Violent behaviour appears to be significantly correlated with persecutory delusions, but not with command hallucinations (Cheung *et al.*, 1997).

Voice hearers' reactions to voices are varied, including fighting back or submission and powerlessness. Romme *et al.* (1992) found that reaction styles were related to the stage that voice hearers are in. Voice hearers who attribute more power to their voices and who assign them higher social status scored higher on subjective suffering, shame and depression on the Beck Depression Inventory. The power persons/individuals attribute to AVHs is related to their social class: the lower persons perceive their own social position the more power they attribute to their voices (Birchwood *et al.*, 2004).

Benjamin (1989) suggests that the social relationship of voice hearers to their voice(s) serves an adaptive function. He supposes a direct relationship between this adaptive function and the chronicity of the disorder. Voices of violent patients had a significantly more negative tone and content compared with those of non-violent subjects. Voices of violent subjects also induced negative emotions more frequently. Characteristics of the voices such as frequency, duration, volume and realism did not discriminate between groups. No relation was found between violent behaviour and command hallucinations. On the other hand, violent voice hearers had more paranoid delusions that made them angry. These persons experienced their coping behaviour as less effective (Cheung *et al.*, 1997).

Prevalence and incidence rates of auditory verbal hallucinations

Incidence rates of AVHs show two peaks. The first is around 18 and 19 years old and the other around 40–49. In females the highest incidence rates are around 20. The second peak occurs in males around their 27th year, while women have their second peak around their 44th year. A significant correlation between AVHs and the manifestation of schizophrenia in adolescence was found by Mueser *et al.* (1989) only. In a French first-tier school study, 16% of the pupils experienced AVHs without having a psychiatric diagnosis (Verdoux *et al.*, 1998). A fairly high AVH prevalence rate was found among American college students: 71% reported having heard AVHs at least once a year, while 61% reported hearing AVHs calling their name in various circumstances once to twice a year (Barrett and Etheridge, 1992). In another study, over 15 000 North Americans were interviewed with the Diagnostic Interview Schedule. In this sample, a 2.3% one-year AVH prevalence rate was calculated. In 50% of this group, no psychiatric diagnosis could be made (Eaton *et al.*, 1991). Two-thirds of these subjects were not bothered by their AVHs (Tien, 1991). In my Dutch unpublished population study a 6% lifetime and 3% one-year prevalence were found. AVHs only occurred in 32%, visual hallucinations in 17%, optical hallucinations in 23%, while 27% had hallucinations in more than one modality. Prevalence appeared to be related to gender and age.

Chapter 2

Historical perspectives

The origin of the word hallucination is the Latin verb *halucinari*, which means 'to wander (in the mind)'. Views on hallucinations have changed a great deal. Across the ages most cultures have differentiated hallucinations that are (a) supernatural, divine and normal from those that are (b) abnormal. In ancient times, Greek, Jewish and Muslim traditions attributed hallucinatory experiences to gods and demons (Cohn-Sherbok and Cohn-Sherbok, 1997; Lippman, 1982). According to contemporary psychiatric and psychological definitions, these supranatural experiences are hallucinations.

The choice between different interpretations of anomalous experiences can have important consequences. Visual and somatic hallucinations may be experienced as divine messages by a mystic, or as histrionic symptoms by a Freudian. A third person may have a physiological interpretation, for example, that the experiences are by-products of sleep deprivation or fasting.

Ancient Chinese texts attributed hallucinations to drugs (Li, 1974). The Greek philosopher Plato reported that Socrates heard voices that influenced his decisions. In Greek mythology, hallucinations were usually attributed to deities, muses or demons with malicious dispositions (Cohn-Sherbok and Cohn-Sherbok, 1997). Disciples of Mohammed recorded visions sent to him by the angel Gabriel in the Koran (Lippman, 1982). Until the eighteenth century, hallucinations were often referred to as 'apparitions' and invested with mystical and spiritual significance. The Christian philosopher Augustine (AD 354–430) distinguished between intellectual, imaginative and corporal apparitions. In the Middle Ages, mystics discriminated divine and diabolic experiences on the basis of spiritual subtlety: the greater the disconnect between the felt significance of the experience and its pure empirical sensation, the greater its religious importance. Scholastics, on the other hand, classified experiences as divine or demonic according to their source and content (Bennett, 1978; Jaynes, 1979; Sarbin and Juhasz, 1967). At the end of the fifteenth century, a Roman Catholic monk wrote in the *Malleus Maleficarum* that hallucinatory experiences were the result of witchcraft and punishable by burning at the stake. In the eighteenth century, physicians claimed the right to define apparitions as divine, devilish or otherwise. At that time the French doctor Esquirol (1832) introduced the medical model that gained precedence towards the end of the nineteenth century. After Kraepelin published his nosology, interest in specific symptoms (hallucinations, delusions) shifted to interest in syndromes and disorders (depression, schizophrenia).

In the mid-twentieth century, interest in symptoms returned. Cognitive behaviour therapists treated hallucinations as obsessive thoughts, with interesting effects as documented in some case studies. In the 1980s, Strauss and other scientists postulated that patients develop symptoms in order to cope with reality: symptoms as coping strategies instead of psychopathology only. Most recent developments are neurobiologically oriented, with studies applying neuroimaging techniques for both research and treatment. Transcranial magnetic stimulation (TMS) is an example of this approach.

What does the research tell us?

Perhaps the most important research message is that hallucinating subjects are not dreamers, liars, malingerers or posers. Hallucinations occur in tandem with brain activity in their corresponding sensory modality. Hallucinated sounds and words can be evoked by direct brain stimulation. The temporal lobe is involved in complex vocal hallucinations, especially the temporal planum and the superior temporal gyrus. A number of studies report significant activation in language-related brain areas during AVHs. The superior temporal gyrus is – on average – smaller in voice-hearing patients with schizophrenia (Rajerethinam *et al.*, 2000). Also, AVHs seem to reduce the temporal cortex's capacity to react to external speech.

The temporal planum specifically reacts to human voices, like a kind of predisposition for human communication. TMS modulates temporal brain cortex reactivity on voice hearing both ipsi- and cross-laterally. Passive listening to speech activates mainly the right temporal brain cortex in healthy subjects. A cheerful sound increases this effect more than a cheerful meaning. However, an opposite effect has been found in schizophrenic patients. Their left temporal cortex reacts more strongly than the right side, suggesting a certain kind of attentional preference for speech characteristics such as emotional intonation and innuendo. This is probably due to involvement of the mid-temporal gyrus.

In summary, AVH is related to a neuronal network of several functional domains and specific brain areas. Complex connections have been demonstrated between hearing, language, speech and the temporal cortex, Heschl's gyrus, superior temporal gyrus, Broca's nucleus and motor temporal gyrus. Connections exist between reality testing and the location of the source of sound and temporal planum, attention, anterior and posterior nucleus cingulate areas and the thalamic area. Emotional reactions are linked to amygdala, insula, hippocampal gyrus, whereas memory and recollection are linked to hippocampus and amygdala. Intentionality and self-monitoring are related to motor associative cortex, nucleus anterior cingulate area, prefrontal cortex, ventral striatal and hippocampal areas. Impulse control is related to the orbitofrontal gyrus (Woodruff, 2004).

Stephane *et al.* (2003) identified three types of AVHs: hearing of words, sentences and communication. This tripartate system is based on different levels of language formation: disturbance in formation of words, semantics and speech.

Intriguing domains of further research may be the roles of attribution and intentions. Do voice hearers locate their voices inside or outside their head? Starting from the inner speech hypothesis, one may assume that voice hearers who attribute their voices to themselves have an intact supplementary motor area, but that voice hearers who are convinced of an external causal object are displaying dysfunction. Functional magnetic resonance imaging (fMRI) has revealed that voices located within the head activate brain areas different from those activated by voices located outside of the head.

So far, intentionality has been neglected in studies on coping behaviour. For example, voice hearers frequently listen to music. Their listening may be part of their daily pattern of life. If so, it probably is not coping, but just habit. It becomes coping only when the listening is intentionally applied to affect their voices.

Part 2

The need for hallucination-focused interventions

Chapter 3

Psychosocial interventions

Introduction

Patients who hear voices often seek help to combat their AVHs and the consequences of the hallucinations. This may explain why mental health care is usually unilaterally focused on the negative consequences of AVHs. Therapists often conceptualize AVH as a disturbing symptom. This is a dubious assumption, as will be illustrated in Chapter 4 (Jenner *et al.*, 1998).

Despite the effectiveness of antipsychotic medications and the reduction of some of their side-effects following the introduction of atypical antipsychotics, AVHs remain to a large extent refractory to medication. This is partly accounted for by medication non-compliance, which is about 30% in the first year rising to 70% over time among patients with schizophrenia (Young *et al.*, 1987). Even in the patients who adhere to their medication regimes, 30% will continue to experience AVHs (Johnstone *et al.*, 1991). Hence, medication-refractory AVHs may be assumed to persist in over 50% of voice-hearing patients with schizophrenia. These patients may benefit from newly developed psychosocial interventions. Some therapies, such as psychodynamic, client-centred and most forms of family therapy, have neither been specifically developed for AVH nor has their effectiveness with respect to AVH been properly studied.

It is only in recent decades that specific hallucination-oriented therapies have been developed. Most of these are additionally framed: they are added to other therapies such as medication, necessitating the involvement of more therapists. In contrast, Hallucination-focused Integrative Treatment (HIT) has not been added to, but is integrated with medication, cognitive behavioural therapy (CBT), coping training, family therapy, psychoeducation and rehabilitation. Ideally, all HIT modules should be given by one therapist. For this reason, the discourse on specific voice-hearing therapies will start with HIT.

Effectiveness of psychosocial interventions

So far, only Empowerment therapy, Voice Dialogue therapy and HIT have been developed to specifically target AVH. Although CBT has been developed for psychiatric disorders – depression, anxiety and psychoses – positive effects on hallucinations have been reported for individual and group CBT. Randomized controlled trials (RCT) have been carried out to determine the effectiveness of CBT and HIT only; the effectiveness of Empowerment and Voice Dialogue rests on case reports. Other psychosocial interventions have been developed for treatment of categorical disorders, such as PTSD, schizophrenia spectrum, dissociative disorder and borderline personality disorder. Psychosocial interventions complement and augment the effect of medication. With respect to psychosis, the meta-analysis by Mojtabai *et al.* (1998) demonstrated the superiority of medication combined with psychosocial interventions over single-component therapies. Psychoeducation and cognitive family therapy programmes uniquely diminish relapse and rehospitalization rates among patients with schizophrenia by 20% (Dyck *et al.*, 2000; Hogarty *et al.*, 1991; McFarlane *et al.*, 1995a, 1995b; Pilling *et al.*, 2002; Pitschel-Walz *et al.*, 2001). Brief family therapy applying psychoeducation only was inferior to a full family therapy programme, and psychodynamic family therapy was found to be ineffective (Dixon and Lehman, 1995). Although the effectiveness of rehabilitation can be improved by integrating it with other forms of treatment (Liberman *et al.*, 1998; Marder, 1999), little evidence suggests that people with schizophrenia ever apply the skills taught in training programmes to real-life situations (Heinssen *et al.*, 2000). The effectiveness of psychosocial interventions may be context dependent, for it appears to be greatest in Western countries (the UK and the Netherlands).

The relevance of psychosocial interventions to psychiatric disorders is beyond dispute. But it is difficult to compare interventions due to variations in experimental design, patient demographics and diagnoses, and the content, comprehensiveness, intensity and duration of the interventions being evaluated (Dickerson, 2000; Gould *et al.*, 2001).

It is clear that therapists and voice hearers have a far from easy task in selecting the 'best' therapy. First, the above-mentioned therapies differ in their goals: CBT focuses on changing attributions, Empowerment and Voice Dialogue aim at understanding the voices and their origin, whereas reduction of subjective burden and social disabilities is pivotal in HIT. Second, the causal focus in CBT is psychosis, especially schizophrenia, while trauma and dissociation are the foci in Empowerment and Voice Dialogue. HIT, in contrast, applies a more pragmatic approach that systematically examines all possible explanations and selects the one(s) that is (are) acceptable for all involved. Third, therapies need to be framed to the individual patient and his or her social network. Fourth, although CBT has the strictest treatment protocol of all, the original Beck CBT protocol has changed over time into an umbrella of various interventions. Some CBT therapists apply techniques known in hypnotherapy, others apply elements from mindfulness, while the application of relaxation exercises and rehabilitation is at random. In other words CBT is CBT, but is not. This complicates the interpretation of CBT effectiveness studies. For example, the meta-analysis carried out for the UK National Institute for Clinical Excellence (NICE, 2011) included HIT results as CBT results, although HIT is quite different from CBT. As mentioned earlier, HIT applies an integrative framework whereas the other therapies use an additive model.

Although no studies comparing CBT, HIT, Empowerment and Voice Dialogue have been done to date, the standard mean differences (SMD), effect sizes (ES) and numbers needed to treat (NNT) of CBT and HIT are compared in Table 3.1. Reasonable effects are: ES of .50 and above, NNT below 10 and SMD not equal to zero. The greater the ES, the lower the NNT and an SMD farther away from zero, the better the results.

The art of integrating therapeutic interventions

In his meta-analysis of psychosocial treatments for schizophrenia, Mojtabai *et al.* (1998) concluded that monotherapies were less effective than combinations of treatment. Inherent in combinations is the choice between the addition of interventions from other programmes and the integration of these interventions. Medical systems, insight-oriented therapies, learning theory and behaviour treatment,

Table 3.1 Comparing the effectiveness of both CBT and HIT versus TAU, as found in RCTs (Luteijn and Jenner, 2012; NICE, 2011)

Effectiveness on	CBT	HIT
Sum of positive symptoms	ES = 0.64	ES = 0.64
	SMD = –0.35	SMD = –1.0
Hallucinations	ES = 0.30	ES = 0.71
	NNT >7	NNT = 2
Duration of effect upon follow-up	+/–	++/–
Hallucination characteristics		
Frequency	+	++
Distress	Unknown	SMD = –0.40
Control	Unknown	SMD = –0.6
Imperative power	Unknown	SMD = –0.86
Compliant with imperatives	SMD = –1.18	Substantial
Malevolence	SMD = –0.97	Substantial
Omniscient	SMD = –0.18	Substantial
Duration of effect upon follow-up	+	+
Depression	NNT unknown	NNT = 4
Anxiety	NNT unknown	NNT = 4
Total burden (AHRS)	SMD = –0.25	Substantial
Duration of effect upon follow-up	SMD = –0.24	SMD = –0.52
Social functioning	Equivocal results	Good (NNT = 6)
Duration of effect upon follow-up	Unknown	++ (significant)
Quality of life	+	++ (significant)
Generalization of effects	Limited	Substantial
Drop-out rate	Medium–high >20%	Low 9%
Patient satisfaction with treatment	Equivocal	Good–very good

SMD, standard mean difference; NNT, number needed to treat; ES, effect size.

rehabilitation, psychoeducation, and general systems theories refer to different models of cause, care and illness (Jenner and Tromp, 1998; Siegler and Osmond, 1966). For example, medical and psychodynamic models attribute no causal role to patients in becoming ill. In contrast, CBT, being based on a moral model, postulates that illness results from the wrong behaviour applied at the wrong time or in wrong situations. This implies that disorders are causally related to the patient's behaviour. Medical, psychiatric and psychological treatments aim at recovery, which is not the primary goal of rehabilitation. Inherent in the addition of models is the inclusion of inherent differences. These may give rise to conflicts in prioritization and the timing of interventions, as well as in therapists' authorities and so on. For example, regular psychiatric and CBT practices label voice hearing as psychotic symptoms and voices as hallucinations. In contrast, Empowerment and Voice Dialogue therapies label voices as 'normal', 'trauma-related' meaningful coping. HIT, on the other hand, may selectively choose the label that is acceptable to all involved in order to reduce drop-out and enhance cooperation. Labelling voices hypercongruently as a gift, as is sometimes done in HIT on specific indication, may conflict with a psychopathological label.

Some therapists ethically doubt hypercongruent interventions. I vote in favour of them given specific circumstances. For example, the patient (Peter) we describe in the section on Motivational strategies below had been unsuccessfully treated with a congruent approach, from an orthodox psychopathology basic assumption. Neither psychoeducation nor convincing and confrontation had been effective. They had only resulted in a request for civil commitment. In such cases, labelling symptoms as gifts may be the only alternative for joining in, for allowing access to the patient's (delusional) system. As our case illustrates, the hypercongruent label opened the way for cooperation and helped to avoid civil commitment.

Initially, interventions, even just monitoring, may lead to exacerbation of voices. Problems may arise when one therapist labels the exacerbation as relapse and another therapist suggests the possibility that this may be the start of 'the voices' death struggle'. The former therapist will decide to stop the monitoring, while the latter will suggest the opposite.

Similarly, extending the interval between sessions, as is described in the section on Selective operant conditioning, may come up against a wall of resistance because common practice is to reduce the interval, while HIT therapists may indicate its extension. Even when extending has been done carefully and purposefully, resistance may remain.

Overcoming the above-mentioned inherent conflicts of addition is an important component of integrative therapies. HIT interventions emanate from different models. Hence, these interventions cannot be simply added up without proper adjustments. In conclusion, HIT cannot be anything but integrative and tailor-made. It requires the tailor to be experienced in various diagnostic systems, styles of communication and methods of intervention.

Chapter 4

Hallucination-focused Integrative Treatment

I invite you to join me in some case vignettes that will give you an impression of the complexity, comprehensiveness, pragmatic creativity of and pleasure to be had in HIT. Time and again I will invite you to make your own plan before reading further about the HIT approach.

Case vignette: Joan (aged 9 years)

Joan's school social worker asked for information about voice hearing. For quite some time, Joan's social behaviour had been changed. She had become quiet and withdrawn, and was performing worse at school, and misbehaved at home. When asked for reasons, she said that she was seeing and hearing two angels: one commanding her to beat her grandfather, the other telling her not to do so. This confused and troubled her. *What would you advise the social worker?*

HIT aims at destigmatization as much as possible. Unfortunately, psychiatric contacts and certainly treatment for psychosis are in themselves unintentionally stigmatizing.

Because of this, we decided not to see the girl unless she appeared to be at serious risk. We suggested the social worker should ask Joan contextual questions and should probe carefully for psychosis and sexual harassment.

It appeared that her grandfather, a widower, had reduced contacts with Joan since he had met a new girlfriend. In the absence of alarming signs, it was concluded that the angels possibly represented Joan's ambivalence about her relationship with her grandfather, whom she both loves and is angry at. In an empathic way Joan was counselled to phone or write to her grandpa telling him that she missed him. After grandpa's positive response, the visions and voices disappeared.

This case illustrates a low profile congruent approach aimed at normalization of voice hearing. The next case illustrates the use of Socratic reasoning and in-depth screening for environmental context and psychopathology aimed at restoring normality in a broad sense.

Case vignette: Mirthe (aged 8 years)

Mirthe's mother contacted me after a TV show about voice-hearing children. For quite some years, Mirthe had had aggressive outbursts, was forgetful, had problems with social contact and was teased at school. According to her mother, the teasing was due to other children envying Mirthe because of her paranormal gifts that had been manifest since the age of 2. *What is your impression? Which questions are relevant? And who do you invite for the intake session?*

Her father, an international trucker, rarely was at home. Mirthe and her mother had a very close relationship (e.g. Mirthe still slept in the conjugal bed). Another close connection existed between her twin sisters. I suspected two camps: Mirthe and mother versus father and the twin sisters, and sensed some tension and conflicts between both camps. *What would you do?*

In contrast with the previous case, I suggested a family intake, which is common practice in HIT. Mirthe's mother strongly objected: her husband had no time, and she did not want to burden the twins. *How do you react?*

I complimented her for making a firm stand for her family, but raised doubts as well, and suggested that exclusion might be stressful for the twins. I also emphasized the need for the father's attendance. At last she agreed to one family assessment session. You may have noticed that I deliberately did not confront her.

During the family intake no psychopathology was found in Mirthe, except her impertinence. Mother and Mirthe were talkative, the others listened without interrupting, but certainly communicated non-verbally. Father clearly disagreed when mother mentioned the paranormal gifts; according to him, mother spoiled Mirthe. However, in reaction to my further questioning he accused psychiatrists of 'only believing in medication'. At the same time he rejected any form of paranormality. *How would you continue?*

I changed attention by focusing on the twins. It appeared that Mirthe dominated her twin sisters. She got her way, and if not went to her mother to tell on the twins. Most of the time, mother took sides with her, blaming the twins and saying that, as older sisters, they should be wiser. Moreover, they were told that Mirthe was not to be blamed – it was her voices. Hence, the twins had to console Mirthe instead of fighting her. The twins were even blamed when defending themselves against Mirthe's temper tantrums and physical assaults, which according to mother were voice-induced too. *How would you proceed?*

My conclusions were that: (a) the parents strikingly disagree (paranormal versus being spoiled), (b) my congruent questions and comments make them stick to the paranormal explanation, (c) Mirthe is being spoiled, (d) there is selective reinforcement of AVH, (e) the family pathology requires Socratic questioning, (f) the mother's conviction with regard to Mirthe's paranormal talent blocks congruent communication, hence a more hypercongruent communication is indicated.

Asked for her first voice-hearing memory, Mirthe said she encountered at least one thousand voices by the age of 2, but she appeared unable to answer any of the Auditory Vocal Hallucination Rating Scale (AVHRS) questions (Appendix 1). This raised some parental doubt about her reliability, as did questions about her development, which appeared to have been normal-to-late.

The mother's conviction made me refrain from further congruent questioning about the voices. I decided to take the 'thousand voices' literally; not in a conclusive (aggressive) way, but in an indirect way hoping to raise some doubt about Mirthe's paranormality.

I expressed my astonishment and asked at what age she became able to add and subtract. This created confusion, and father accused me of psychiatric prejudice. He insisted I should believe that bad spirits possessed Mirthe at the age of 2: she banged her head, foamed at the mouth and did not react to her parents. Mirthe, continuing on the subject of her visions, said they *must* be ghosts. I elaborated on the relevance of discriminating bad from good spirits; all agreed. Next, they were given monitoring homework. Finally, I gave psychoeducation on selective reinforcement, bad spirits being afraid of effective coping strategies, and on strong personalities.

Mirthe expected to need at least 5 more years before becoming strong enough to stop sleeping in the conjugal bed. I relabelled her reluctance as well considered and explained to her parents both the advantages of behaving in accordance with age, and the disadvantages of enduring childish behaviour. At the next session, monitoring showed some parental changes. Two months later, the voices had disappeared, normal behaviour was being reinforced and Mirthe was sleeping in her own bed.

Now, I have no knowledge about the cause(s) of change. Was it treatment? The mother's new 32 hours per week appointment? Or just a lucky coincidence?

Both these cases ended up well. Let us now follow some severely psychotic voice hearers. As you will have noticed, preparing the session and creating surprise are common practice in HIT. Another condition is sufficient time. The mean duration of sessions is 60–90 minutes, but HIT-based crisis intervention sessions may take 2 hours. This seems quite a long time, but is short in relation to the total duration of treatment and its results.

Case vignette: Mrs Benson

The police requested civil commitment for Mrs Benson (aged 46 years), a single mother of three, with a prior history of three civil commitments. Her youngest son had been removed from the maternal home and lived at his schoolteacher's house due to child neglect. Delusions caused the patient to accuse her neighbours of sexual abuse and of throwing bricks into her mailbox. In response, she had refused to allow the family doctor to enter the house to treat her severely diabetic mother. All kinds of treatment had been offered, but she refused any help. Neighbours called in the police regularly. The police requested civil commitment on the grounds that her neighbours were seriously planning to take revenge. By accident the request reached the HIT team, instead of the crisis intervention unit. *What would your plan of action be?*

We constructed the following plan of action: (1) Because of her known preference for men, a male psychiatrist will make a home visit. (2) We will search for whatever complaint for which she wants help. (3) Indirect communication will be made with the patient through her mother, which implies making the home visit when the mother is at home. (4) We will wait for the right moment to introduce interventions. (5) We will prepare for hypercongruency.

At the door, I offered the patient help in removing the (non-existent) bricks. She thanked me and invited me to come inside. She paced back and forth and up and down, talking incoherently about her neighbours' sexual harassment. Communication with her mother appeared impossible. Mrs Benson explained that she rejected medication because of its bitter taste. She repeated that she had no need for help. Eventually, after quite some discussion she agreed I could help her to get feel and behave with more self-confidence and to gain improvement of her social functions. It struck me that she repeatedly bowed her head and wrapped her arms around herself. When asked to explain her gestures, she told me that a black bird was trying to peck her skin. This seemed the right moment for action. Joining in seemed most appropriate. First, I feigned anger and called this bird's behaviour outrageous and unacceptable. Next I asked her to protect me: 'Please warn me when the birds attack me.' She promised to do so. I then Socratically suggested that birds may not like bitter foods, and challenged her to take the bitter medication in order to deter the birds. She reacted unexpectedly: 'I smell of a grave. Can't you smell it?' I was stunned, and did not know what to say. *Would you reply and if so what would you say?*

Her dirty feet offered me a flash of inspiration: 'Could it be your feet? They are dirty. Could you please wash them?' A debate between mother and patient ensued. The patient refused because ghosts prevented her from entering the bathroom. Again, I feigned anger and asked her permission to try to send the ghosts away, which she accepted. After having made some gestures and mumbled some words I invited her to screen the bathroom for ghosts. No more could be detected. After I had washed her feet (why not?), she took medication and invited me to return for a second visit. This first home visit took 2 hours. I made daily visits thereafter, and on the 5th day she opened the door washed, clean and well dressed and poured me tea.

Total therapy time, including travelling and team consultation, accounted for 8 hours and 45 minutes. Of course, she needed further aftercare so I saw her weekly and we discussed problems and controlled her medication. She recovered within three months. One year later the AVHs had gone and the medication could be cut down and stopped the next year. She has not remitted since.

Case vignette: Mrs Fence

Mrs Fence's family doctor and husband requested urgent crisis intervention for her. Some weeks ago, this 38-year-old, friendly, good mother of two and wife had become psychotic. She heard the voice of President George W. Bush, ordering her to go to Kabul. He spoke to her through the radiator, TV, and other equipment. She was absolutely convinced that the USA needed her for secret operations against the Taliban. Since then, she had neglected her household and children. Her day–night rhythm had changed. She demanded that her husband should arrange an airline ticket and apply for a visa; she did not accept any delay, and was not afraid of physical action. She was not susceptible to any argument, nor would she listen to reason. *Please, make your plan of action.*

(continued)

(continued)

Based upon the ineffectiveness of former congruent interventions, surprise and hypercongruency were chosen as cores.

After her lengthy, delusional explanations, I asked her whether she had ever been in Asian Muslim countries, which she had not. I then told her about my 2-year stay in India, with some emphasis on feminine roles. Next, I asked her to tell me about what she expected to experience in Kabul. She did not know. I asked her whether she might be interested to hear my expectations. She was. My next question about whether she had purchased a Niqab or Burka clearly surprised her. I explained that she would be put in jail with her Western fancy clothes, and would be treated as a whore and exposed on TV as such. Probably, the Taliban would use her to campaign against Bush. Had she ever considered this possibility? She had not. Furthering this pathway, I tried to insert doubt by asking her about the chances that the CIA, FBI and military intelligence would not know these consequences of her going to Kabul. Next, I proposed the possibility that Taliban forces had misled her by sending false messages in the name of Bush, and if so could she possibly deteriorate his position? To cut a long story short, at the end she agreed to postpone her flight and do some more investigations at the American embassy. She accepted haloperidol as empowering medication against possible Taliban influences.

This hypercongruent intervention could postpone the crisis, but further intensive treatment was needed for quite some time.

The HIT format

In adolescents and adults the HIT programme consists of 15 (mean) 1 hour sessions over 9–12 months (Jenner, 2002, 2012). The median duration of HIT is 9 months with a median of 11 sessions. Variations in duration (SD 9) and contacts (SD 12) can be large if need persists. All sessions are conducted as single-family interventions. In middle childhood and pre-adolescent children the means are five sessions in a four month period.

Treatment focuses on the patient 'taking back control of his or her head'. HIT is delivered according to a protocol delineated in a manual which is routinely tailored to the individual patient. This means that specific elements may vary in duration or intensity (Jenner, 2012a, 2012b). Operant conditioning is applied to increase adherence.

Patients are advised to involve relevant others in their treatment. If the patient agrees, family members are invited to participate in sessions as much as they can.

Table 4.1 The HIT format

Programme	15 1-hour sessions (mean) adolescents and adults
	5 1.5-hour sessions (mean) children
Duration	9–12 months (mean) adolescents and adults
	2–4 months children
Contents	Directive treatment approach
	Systems orientation and treatment
	Outreach crisis intervention 24/7
	Integration of various interventions
Modules	Two-realities principle
	Seeking a workable reality acceptable for all
	Selective motivational strategies
	Medication
	Training patient and key figures in coping
	CBT
	Symptom-oriented psychoeducation
	Rehabilitation in terms of coping

The format is comprehensive (Table 4.1). Searching for a therapeutic alliance with patient *and* key figures is pivotal. HIT aims to achieve a workable reality that is acceptable for all involved. Mutual consent prevails over the correctness or validity of causal models and diagnoses. This feature of HIT can be justified by the simple fact that evidence for current causal models of hallucinations is weak, but is also logical because cooperation yields better results than confrontation. Mutual consent even prevails over a correct DSM classification.

The hospital-centred organization has been replaced by a customer-oriented approach guided by the slogan 'the customer is always right'. Guided by this principle, my outpatients psychiatric clinic has been renamed the 'Voice Hearer's Clinic' and the children's outpatients department is called AUDITO (from the Esperanto).

The programme includes psychiatric diagnosis, and assessment of hallucinations, habitual styles of behaviour and systems dynamics. Interventions have been selected on evidence and best-practice criteria. They include: (1) two-realities principle, (2) motivational strategies, (3) medication, (4) training patient and relatives in coping strategies, (5) cognitive behavioural interventions, (6) symptom-oriented psychoeducation and (7) rehabilitation. They represent medical, biological, genetic, interactional, social, spiritual and moral models. The treatment style is a combination of directive problem solving and Socratic reasoning (Box 4.1).

Box 4.1 Socratic reasoning

Socratic reasoning is about the opposite of confrontation. The Socratic interviewing style seeks to give as little direct advice to the patient as possible and does not focus on proving the therapist is right and the voice hearer is wrong. Rather it seeks to elicit suggestions for change and solutions from the voice hearer. Preferably the therapist helps or seduces the patient to draw his or her own doubt with an indirect style of disputing and testing the patient's inferences about the power of his or her AVHs (Chadwick and Birchwood, 1996). Questions such as 'Is it possible that . . . ?' 'Have you considered . . . ?' 'What do you think of . . . ?' have proved their effectiveness.

All is embedded in a framework of systems treatment with outreach crisis intervention available 24/7 if needed. Diagnosis and interventions are not strictly separated. Interventions that are implemented during the diagnostic stage include ways of conducting interviews, framing questions, application of Socratic reasoning, (positive) reframing of answers, semantic conditioning, and summarizing in terms that may raise doubts. Simply assessing voices with the AVHRS (see Appendix 1; Jenner and van de Willige, 2002) induces re-attribution of AVH in many patients. HIT modules are implemented according to individual needs and preferences, stage of motivation and a patient's personality structure. Indicators for selecting the appropriate strategy are patient, voices and family histories, meaning of and attribution to voices, anxiety level, and explanations regarding origin of voices.

Adding or integrating interventions and models of care

HIT integrates the two-realities principle, motivating strategies, coping training, family therapy, CBT, medication, psychoeducation, rehabilitation and crisis intervention. This entails a mandatory need for integration of the above-mentioned models of care as well as integration with regard to timing and phasing of the various HIT modules. HIT prefers a tailor-made order of the modules. Alongside this flexibility, protocols have been created for each module:

- Stage 1 aims at making contact and preserving it. Explanation of the HIT method, diagnosis, organization of monitoring and the making of a crisis plan are pivotal.
- Stage 2 involves psychoeducation, discussion about medication and structuring a personal coping plan.
- Stage 3 aims at finishing HIT and the preparation of a personal relapse-prevention programme (see Appendix 7). This includes a written document about detection of early symptoms, effective coping strategies, parameters for controlling the process for and responsibilities of patient and key figures and a crisis scenario in case of crisis.

All persons involved sign the prevention programme, which is sent to the family doctor and all specialists involved.

During all stages, attitudinal and motivational rules remain valid, as does the continuous testing of action proneness with the illness-awareness cycle of Prochaska and DiClemente (1982). Homework is started as soon as possible. Most of the time homework has been given at intake, because many voice hearers have insufficient knowledge about the frequency and contextual aspects of their voices. Form and content of monitoring are adjusted to the stage of treatment. Starting with contextual fact gathering, the monitoring changes as treatment proceeds to effect measurement of coping strategies. The need for cognitive interventions rises with the delusional component of the voices.

Psychoeducation, rehabilitation and empowerment stem from the compensation model that teaches acceptance of and dealing with handicaps. Although coping training aims at dealing as well, it aims more at recovery than at acceptance. As mentioned before, CBT and medication share the goal of healing. The former is based on the learning theory and the latter on physiology and genetics. Siegler and Osmond (1966) distinguish two medical models: the business model and the own responsibility model. In the first model medical specialists are in control; they renew and adjust deficient components while patients pass by as if on a conveyor belt. In the second model the patient remains in control, and therapists deliver the wanted goods. The second medical model fits the moral models better than the first.

Different models imply different professional jargons, ethics, knowledge and skills. Also, during training some professional differentiation occurs, resulting in professional domains: psychiatrists for physical examination, medication and a decisive role in civil commitment procedures, psychologists for CBT, psychiatric nurses for rehabilitation, and so on. At least these legally laid down qualifications are related to decisional leadership in respective domains which may result in competition.

It will be clear that addition without readjustments may result in situations of conflict (e.g. about priorities) in treatment programmes. Proper adjustments with regard to attitude, management of therapeutic processes and priorities, collaboration within teams, and resolving conflicts that are inherent to combining different treatment programmes are mandatory elements of integration. As a result it may be easier for one therapist to deliver the integrative programme HIT than several therapists in an added up combination programme. Limiting the number of therapists per patient has the advantage of being less confusing for patients, certainly for patients with schizophrenia with their disturbed verbal memory and face recognition, or for those with borderline personalities who tend to act-out and play therapists off against each other, or for patients with autism.

At first, therapists may find it difficult to integrate the various modules into an effective and feasible programme that is acceptable for the patient. Hence, training and supervision are mandatory. The Dutch HIT network provides such a programme.

Tailor-made or theory-driven interventions?

Disturbed reality testing, lack of insight and cognitive deficits in voice hearers are pivotal in psychiatry. Emphasizing these deficiencies and confronting voice hearers with their reality testing are seemingly logical interventions when one considers that non-compliance and resistance are disease related. However, voice hearers *hear* their voices, as neuroimaging has demonstrated. Hence, they feel personally rejected by a confrontational approach (Cohen and Berk, 1985). Voice hearers deserve therapists who are willing to listen to the strange experiences they themselves do not understand, can neither explain nor effectively articulate, and may find scary, certainly in the beginning. The more therapists focus on convincing voice hearers that they are mentally disordered, the more patients will feel misunderstood and that their experiences are being neglected. The more confrontational the therapist becomes, the greater the patient's denial. From this perspective, patient non-compliance is a disastrous reaction to an unproductive therapeutic approach. Theory-obedient therapists may unintentionally increase delusional thinking processes. Similar results may come from accepting psychotic voices without comment. HIT tries to solve this dilemma by a tailor-made treatment that flexibly integrates consumer needs and belief systems with theory-based facts and evidence-based interventions adjusted to habitual patterns of behaviour.

Intake

Neither diagnosis nor treatment can start without a therapeutic relationship. Unfortunately, many voice hearers have a dislike for psychiatry. The question is whether this is disease-related or relation-bound. Studies report a 30–70% treatment/medication non-compliance rate among voice hearers with psychiatric disorders (Young et al., 1987). Confronting voice hearers with their disturbed reality testing and psychoeducation sessions about cognitive deficits, preferably given with conviction, are seemingly logical interventions for therapists who consider non-compliance to be disease-related in terms of lacking insight, disturbed reality testing, or resistance. In contrast, HIT therapists who interpret non-compliance as (partly) interpersonal, prefer motivational interviewing, relabelling and reframing to confrontation. Because HIT aims to achieve a workable reality acceptable to all, the psychiatric outpatient clinic has been renamed as 'voice hearers' clinic'.

From the very beginning, activities focused on building and maintaining a working relationship are applied. To achieve an effective working alliance, it may help to keep the following points in mind:

- Voice hearers often have an antipathy to mental health-care workers and psychiatric treatment.
- It is important to accept that voice hearers hear voices.
- The therapist should aim at a workable reality, rather than at a dogmatic reality.

- A stepwise diagnostic protocol should be used.
- Socratic reasoning about AVH should be applied as the preferred style of communication.

HIT intakes start with involving patients by asking them what they prefer. Do they want to start with telling their stories? Do they have urgent questions? Do they want us to start, for example, with information about voice hearing, or an explanation of HIT? By doing so we illustrate our willingness to share, negotiate and cooperate, also the possibilities for change and adjustment. Last but not least, this approach 'seduces' the voice hearer to play an active role in his or her treatment. We have noticed this to be pivotal in enhancing cooperation and reducing non-compliance and drop-outs.

The two-realities principle

The goal of the two-realities principle is to facilitate therapeutic bonding that would be nullified by poorly timed confrontation. Voice hearers often feel ignored and invalidated when therapists doubt the reality of their hallucinated experiences (Cohen and Berk, 1985). We emphasize the need for detailed assessment of the AVHs. HIT therapists explicitly state that AVHs are accepted as real experiences of voice hearers.

In HIT there are at least *two realities*, one of which is the patient's. The patient is an expert on his or her reality and responsible for his or her actions. In line with this slogan, AVHs are accepted as real experiences. This is both a sign of good salesmanship and of applied science, as imaging studies illustrate synchronicity of AVH and neurons firing in the Broca and Wernicke's areas of the brain (David, 1999; Stephane *et al.*, 2001; Weiss and Heckers, 1999). The other reality is that *I* do not actually hear voices. This makes voice hearers experts compared to therapists in terms of subjective experience. When voice hearers accept this 'two-realities reality', and most of them eventually do, they also indirectly and implicitly take on the role of an 'experienced expert' and the responsibilities that go with this title. Then, therapists explicitly call voice hearers to account for their expert role.

We have found this 'experienced expert' role has great consequences in terms of less negativism and more patient willingness to independently monitor AVH characteristics, their consequences, and their relatives' behaviour too. It also has been our experience that this elevation of the patient to the role of 'expert' improves cooperation and compliance with homework tasks.

Consequences of causal concept ordering

The next step in bonding is the sharing of patient, relatives and therapist – in this order – in the identification of as many causes and explanations of voice hearing as possible. Each person's causes are then ordered by their relative likelihood or credence and discussed in turn by all involved. This process appears to make patients more willing to accept non-psychotic explanations. Each participant is requested to connect his or her explanations with logical plans of action, for which duration, responsibilities for implementation and parameters of success are decided. Responsibilities for psychotic explanations and related plans of action are left with the patient, who is kept as much as possible to the agreed upon responsibilities and timing. Therapists may apologize for having insufficient knowledge of the supranatural or the spirits. However, HIT therapists take an active role in processes regarding other causes. For example, trauma may be connected with a period of mourning and work-out, witchcraft with rituals, and diseases and illnesses with medication and psychotherapy. Christians who are convinced that their voices come from the devil or are God's punishment for their sins may start prayer and psalm singing, Hindus may do puja, and Muslims read sura. Finally, therapist, patient and relatives discuss the feasibility of each plan of action. Some intriguing consequences of this stepped approach have been noticed. Patients accept other explanations, including the therapist's, rather than their own only, and appear to accept relatively easily the testing of both psychotic and non-psychotic plans of action. This leads to better cooperation and compliance, while resistance and drop-out decrease. Some patients determine certain delusion-driven plans of action as being unfeasible and independently withdraw them.

Tailoring HIT

Tailoring entails properly adjusting the programme to what is expected to be most effective in a particular patient. For example, narcissistic persons easily stand up against authority. Hence, they may respond better (seemingly?) if given command in therapy by being offered choices instead of being given direct advice. These choices are given within the boundaries of the intended plan of action. A narcissistic patient may be given advice on medication as paradoxical choices. They are not between yes or no, but between which antipsychotic at what time in what dose. The patient's narcissistic traits may be 'used'; for example by suggesting that homework exercises are possibly too difficult. Narcissists usually cannot but show the therapist to be mistaken.

In contrast, direct and concrete pieces of advice may be better for intellectually disabled or autistic patients. Schizophrenia is preferably made pivotal in treating a member of a schizophrenia association, and a distant approach chosen because of their cluster A personality structure. In contrast, early traumatic experiences may be given preference in a patient who is a member of Intervoice, a voice hearers' association that challenges psychiatric diagnoses and believes in trauma-related meanings of voices. This patient is treated emphatically, and a permissive style anticipates his or her possible borderline ambivalence regarding responsibility. Cultural and religious differences dictate other approaches: a Moroccan patient may be asked what Moroccan psychiatrists would suggest, or a Turkish patient asked about Turkish approaches. If rejection of medication is expected they are advised to let Allah demonstrate which medication is the preferred one. One of my Hindu patients claiming to be Lord Krishna was asked to prove this by turning blue, which is Krishna's colour.

Less is more

Patients with schizophrenia may suffer cognitive handicaps in verbal memory and face recognition. It may be argued that the greater the number of therapists involved in their treatment, the more these handicaps become noticeable (Jenner, 2008a, 2010). Pursuing this reasoning, patients may benefit from as few therapists as possible and, conversely, may suffer from multidisciplinary teams with shared caseloads. HIT's rule of thumb reads 'less is more', which implies that HIT is best administered by one therapist, who also prescribes any medication too. Consultations are singular and preferably done in the presence of the primary therapist. Another expression of the 'less is more' rule is that, except for dangerous situations, therapies are usually better ended when the patient is satisfied with the results, even if this is against the therapist's opinion.

The strong relation between non-compliance and dissatisfaction is clear: HIT therapists have noticed a fairly good return of satisfied patients to treatment.

Preference for one therapist for full treatment is another aspect of less is more. Knowing that cognitive deficits in face recognition and word remembrance are common in patients with schizophrenia, this preference is hardly surprising.

Motivational strategies

Non-compliance is far from exceptional but is the rule in voice hearers with psychiatric disorders. Patient-bound assumptions about their lack of motivation neglect communicative aspects of motivation. This easily gives rise to self-fulfilling prophesies that ultimately result in therapeutic stagnation. In contrast, treatment implies the creation of conditions leading to beneficial changes. Therapists' attitudes and skills determine this creative process to a great extent. Hence, HIT prefers Miller and Rolnick's (1991) definition of motivation as a state of readiness or eagerness to change. This highlights the impact of context-dependent fluctuations that allow for various motivation-focused interventions that are less patient dependent. HIT applies various motivating strategies, both direct and indirect, and of a congruent as well as hypercongruent nature; congruent when possible, hypercongruent if needed. Direct explanations as to how and why voice hearing occur and interventions, and about expected consequences are examples of congruent communication. Explaining internal speech and fMRI findings as causes of voice hearing are congruent interventions.

Hypercongruent communication may be indicated when a congruent approach does not work. This may occur in some psychotic states, especially the deluded ones and also in cases of severe ambivalence, as may be encountered in cluster

B personality disorders. Then, the therapist may take a patient's words extremely literally. Patients who attack other persons against their will because the devil commands them to do so are advised to pray, read their religious books and sing hymns instead of attacking people. Are their attacks meant to convert unbelievers to God, Allah or one of the Hindu deities? If so, they are questioned about the effectiveness of their attacks and are advised to demonstrate God's, Allah's or Lord Krishna's love by helping people instead of attacking them. We can illustrate this with a case vignette.

Case vignette: Peter

Peter (aged 46 years), an intellectually disabled man with delusions about being poisoned, repeatedly heard voices commanding him to destroy his parents' refrigerator and kitchen. Before consulting the Voices Outpatients Department he had strongly rejected insight-oriented therapy and congruent cognitive behaviour. This, in combination with his severe reality distortion, made me choose a hypercongruent approach. I compared him, a Presbyterian, with the Pharaoh's food taster and labelled his delusion about being poisoned as a kind of talent. He liked the importance of this label. This made him willing and able to replace his delusion-driven destructive behaviour with a more constructive view of protecting his parents from poisoning. He agreed that such talent should be used in helping his mother to pick non-poisoned food in shops. Empathetic Socratic reasoning concerning the risk of civil commitment in reaction to his possible aggressive outbursts in shops when confronted with 'poisoned' food made him willing to take medicine as part of his protective responsibility, because if he were committed he would leave his parents unprotected.

As you will have noticed, the indication for this hypercongruent approach was Peter's absolute rejection of a congruent approach. The hypercongruent approach made him accept responsibility for the consequences of his (psychotic) behaviour, even without accepting any sign of psychosis. This change implied a switch in focus from insight, convincing and wanting to have the last word towards behaviour, responsibility and getting the patient's agreement. In this case, hypercongruency made sense because constantly confronting severely deluded patients with their distorted reality testing may fortify their deluded conviction.

Ambivalent voice hearers, such as patients with histrionic or borderline personality disorder, need therapists able to solve both a patient's opposing needs at the same time, which is impossible. Therapists' advice that regards only one pole of this ambivalence often evokes acting-out behaviour. HIT therapists try to frame advice that preferably deals with both poles. Dealing with this problem may be fairly simple in theory, but complex in practice. First, we give psychoeducation about the two conflicting strivings: hold-me but leave-me. Next, we give two sets of advice, one for each striving. Finally, we suggest that their subconscious should to be able to select the best advice. This may look like deceit, but is not for ambivalent persons.

Psychotic patients may be held responsible hypercongruently in line with their psychotic reasoning, not by confrontation, but by Socratic reasoning. Patients who lack self-care and who believe that deities are ordering them to convert the world may be questioned about the likelihood that their tattered and smelly clothes keep people away from God. Quite a few patients have improved their self-care and hygiene after a debate on how to become an effective advertisement for God. As the reader will have noticed, hypercongruency may open new perspectives. That is its strength.

Motivating patients who avoid contact

Some psychotic symptoms, such as disorganization, paranoia, delusion and incoherence, interfere with normal contacts and communication and hence may require exceptional contact-furthering strategies. These states may require Prouty's pretherapy, indirect communication through third persons, Ferreira's mothering and horror techniques, finding any complaint for which help is accepted, and hypercongruency.

Prouty's reflections

In Prouty's approach, recovery of dysfunctional ego functions is pivotal. The therapist's aim is to function as an external ego by providing reflections directed on reality, feelings and communication. Reflections may concern: situations (e.g. it is cold), affective facial expressions (e.g. you have sad eyes), repetition of words, reflections on or imitations of postures. Reflections that evoke positive or emotional reactions are reiterated. Somatic reflections have been reported to be effective in catatonia and restlessness. The results of Prouty's reflections have not been properly studied yet, but case reports are impressive. Feelings of being mocked and being misunderstood are possible side-effects in paranoid patients, although these complications have not been reported.

Indirect communication through a third person

When direct patient–therapist communication is impossible, communication via a third person may be tried. Reflections about the patient's behaviour and condition are communicated to and through a third person. As much as possible, positive labelling is used. However, horror (see below) may also be applied. Third persons are most often needed in non-communicative patients, mutism and incoherence as well as in the severely mentally ill living alone, and in crises (Jenner, 1984). For these reasons HIT therapists regularly invite key figures to therapy sessions, and go together with trainees to the emergency room, police station and on home visits (Jenner, 2013).

Ferreira's mothering and horror

Ferreira (1959) defined psychotic behaviour as a form of communication. Rejection of help may be interpreted as a psychotic symptom requiring a therapeutic dominant complementary attitude. Simultaneously, but in contradiction, patient civil rights demand a symmetrical attitude, with a risk of negligence. Ferreira's mothering and horror interventions intend to solve this command dilemma by defining communication within a framework of care and concern. Mothering imposes help on the patient and by doing so redefines the relationship as a complementary one. Acceptation of the imposed help implies acceptance of the definition of care, while rejection implies redefinition which also implies communication. This intervention is said to be effective even in patients with catatonia and mutism.

Case vignette: Sheela

Sheela, single, aged 20, was severely drug addicted, promiscuous, talked incoherently or was mutistic. Regularly, police found her in a state of confusion. At the request of her desperate mother, the HIT team made a home visit; Sheela ignored us. Hence, we applied communication via the mother (third person). We relabelled her behaviour as a kind of regression in age. We suggested the mother should care for her daughter in accordance with her 'regressed age', as if she were a toddler. In reaction, Sheela started kicking and screaming with periods of coherent spells. Latter behaviour was directly and consistently reinforced. After over 30 minutes, contact had normalized sufficiently for treatment to be started.

Horror summarizes potential negative (prospective) consequences to the present (back to the future) in order to induce a wish for change. Its motive is caring. It is meant to raise awareness about possible, unwanted consequences of the patient's present behaviour. Certainly, it is neither meant to accuse, blame nor unrealistically scare the patient, nor is it moralistic or pedantic.

Case vignettes: Harold and Mary

Horror made Harold, a schizophrenic, paranoid patient, accept indirectly offered help. In a psychotic state he had pulled out his fingernails, which had become inflamed. Therapists communicated via his mother (third-person communication) and summarized possible consequences, such as blood poisoning and gangrene. He then accepted wound care with disinfectants. An analogy between the working of disinfectants and medication made him accept antipsychotic medication.

Mary, a female psychotic hallucinating patient, was incontinent for urine and faeces. She remained in bed because of deluded fractures. She refused any care. Fear of being poisoned made her refuse drinks: an urgent and dangerous situation. I explained to her husband (third-person communication) the risks of dehydration: thrombosis, bedsores, epileptic insults and pain. Next, I showed the patient my concern and my intention to prevent her from getting these experiences. Simultaneously, I offered her something to drink and requested her – hypercongruently – not to move in order to prevent further fractures. This combination placed her in a paradoxical situation. Movements and knocking away the glass would be motor improvements, while drinking would reduce the risk of dehydration: improvement too. The intervention made her accept drink and helped to prevent civil commitment. Improvement started some time later.

Search for the complaints

Patients who deny being psychotic and reject treatment may be willing to accept help for problems that are not disorder related. The case of Mrs Benson, described above, is an example of searching for a complaint; the patient accepted help in improving her social functioning. Tired or sleepless (psychotic) patients may be interested in fortified medicinal wines (antipsychotics), such as the ones that were fashionable in the 1960s. Paranoid patients may be interested in being shielded against static electric fields by a Faraday's cage, for example. Ask them whether they know about this wire-constructed cage and explain how it protects against radiation. You may get their attention. Then conclude and agree with your patient that such a cage would give the impression of madness. Would they perhaps appreciate a 'chemical cage' with similar protection? If so, prescribe an antipsychotic.

Hypercongruent interventions

Hypercongruent interventions may be used in both patients that reject, as well as those that accept contact. These interventions are described extensively in the next section.

Motivational interventions

Treatment efficacy depends greatly on the quality of the therapeutic relationship. The characteristics of the therapist, patient, overarching society, their relatives and other key figures are pivotal in this relationship. Voice hearers with psychiatric diagnoses are renowned for their aversion to psychiatric help as well as their non-compliance (Cohen and Berk, 1985; Johnstone et al., 1991). Because no therapy will ever be effective in the absence of the patient, the major therapeutic task is getting in touch with the patient and keeping up a good relationship. Hence, motivational strategies are indispensable. HIT applies a broad spectrum of motivational strategies that may help to prevent escalation and to increase treatment compliance.

The art of motivation

Clinical recommendations are an important part of therapy. Our clinical advice is based on our conviction that patient adherence will improve a person's mental, somatic and interpersonal well-being. However, despite our best intentions, patient non-compliance ranges from 20 to 80%. The result is a stalemate between the patient, his or her relatives and the therapist. How do frustrations get so out of hand that they may result in an oppositional relationship? Do we blame the patient, the psychiatric diagnosis, the form or content of our advice, the adviser, or a combination of these variables? More importantly, how do we prevent such outcomes? Frequently, frustration results from disturbed communications due to bad listening and divergent conceptions of treatment goals.

Trust in the therapist and treatment determines therapeutic effectiveness to a great extent. Thirty percent of the variance in therapeutic outcome depends on trust in the therapist and the therapy. To some extent, this trust is a function of therapist characteristics. The personality, treatment style and communication skills of the therapist, including attention, empathy and intonation, are good predictors of compliance. Personal style and good communication are crucial.

Textbooks usually describe non-compliance in negative patient terms: lack of insight, pessimism, motivational deficiency and so on. Is this right? *No.* Why not? First, non-compliance may occasionally be smarter than compliance. There is sufficient evidence that older treatments were harmful in the long term. Think of exorcism, blistering, insulin coma and radiation for tuberculosis. At least in these cases, patient non-compliance would have been good. Even if we restrict the concept of non-compliance to discussions of modern treatment paradigms, we still find that (partial) non-compliance can be a wise decision. Frequent lawsuits against pharmaceutical companies in recent years have raised doubts about their reliability and the effectiveness of various medications. The recent study by Wunderink et al. (2013) showing the long-term positive effects of antipsychotic dose reductions in a number of patients with chronic schizophrenia supports the value of limited medication non-compliance in some cases.

Medication non-compliance is not restricted to psychiatric patients. Except for women and the elderly, no significant correlation has been found between non-compliance, sociodemographic variables and knowledge about diseases. Over 80% of elderly patients with somatic disorders took their prescribed medication irregularly or not at all. These rates may be a partly motivation-related problem (Fawcett, 1999; see also Cramer, 1991; Haynes, 1976; Perkins, 2002).

Lack of motivation is wrongly seen as just a psychiatric disorder-related factor, a negative symptom or a personality trait. These attributions assume that motivation is a trait or stable variable: you have or have not got sufficient motivation. If this were the case, attempting to motivate patients would be a waste of time and money. People who hold this view of motivation better spend less time and money on affecting it. Viewing a lack of motivation as a sickness thus creates a self-fulfilling prophecy.

Creating motivation

Imagine a man entering your fishing shop asking for a special type of bait. How do you respond? 'Yes' or 'no'? Actually, you could consider a third option. You might say: 'Not many people know about that type of bait. Sounds like you really know your stuff. Are you a pro?' The customer may feel flattered. He will probably react enthusiastically. You comment that this bait yields even better results with a new kind of hook. You end up selling the man the perfect reel, the latest float . . . You continue as long as the man shows interest, preferably up until the moment he leaves the shop with a complete new fishing pole. And just before he is leaving your shop you may interest him in a new fishing suitcase. You are the perfect salesman.

Therapists are salesmen too. They sell therapies that improve quality of life, take away causes of disease or at the very least reduce suffering. Like good salesmen, good therapists show interest in their clients, spark discussions, initially interest them in something small and then expand towards other relevant issues. Salesmen hope to see their buyers again, so they refrain from swindling them. They try to send customers home satisfied, with positive feelings. Profit is the ultimate goal of business. It is the hierarchical sequence of ethical values that distinguishes therapists from businessmen. At least I hope so. Otherwise, mental health care faces an enormous problem. Improvement, safety, respect and efficiency are the ultimate goals of therapists. The introduction of market forces with their emphasis on cost-efficiency threatens quality of care by threatening the health orientation of the therapeutic community. The practices outlined in this chapter are designed to respect the old therapeutic ethics.

Therapy aims at changes that ultimately improve a patient's quality of life. Because not all changes are pleasant, resistance is a normal reaction. Lack of information, insecurity, fear of the unknown, disability, habituation to the status quo, laziness, negative self-image and a need for punishment are factors that may impede change. When our patients' ultimate therapeutic goals differ from our own, it is safe to assume a 'diagnosis' of lack of motivation. In such cases, neither psychoeducation nor controlling behaviour will make any difference. Fortunately, motivation is context dependent. People, patients included, are always capable of motivation. Some patients have a characteristically strong motivation not to follow their therapist's advice, irrespective of the content of that advice. It follows that motivation for these patients is also an interactive process. The motivation of our patients is connected (at least in part) to our motivation and motivational skills. This is pleasant on the one hand, for it means that we can bring about change. It may be unpleasant too, as failures can no longer be attributed to the patient alone.

Flexibility is an essential motivational strategy in HIT. Pseudoflexibility runs the risk of total discouragement. A milder form of pseudoflexibility is commenting positively on someone's remark as a means of taking the floor yourself. Pseudoflexibility is discourteous and therapeutically dangerous. It easily creates irritation and increases the risk of drop-out. Therapeutically, I can only imagine two cases where pseudoflexibility is acceptable (and then only with great restraint and as a last resort): (1) extremely talkative people who cannot be stopped by either open forms of communication or confrontation, and (2) cases where 'standard' reactions may reinforce delusional thinking.

Hypercongruence has proven effective in treating patients with psychosis or 'anti-therapeutic personalities'. Hypercongruent methods take a person's expressions literally. For example, if a patient complains about being too fatigued to do homework or follow therapeutic advice, despite being able to watch TV and engage in other pleasant activities, you may advise him to sleep more, preferably in a consequent programme. Take care that sleeping is meant for rest and not for secondary gain. Accepting rest, or worse, suggesting the combination of rest plus pleasant activities not only undermines your advice, it also teaches the patient how to avoid difficult but important tasks on questionable psychological grounds. In other words, such a combination reinforces avoidance behaviour. This advice may sound counter-therapeutic or cruel, but it is not. A really tired person deserves rest, for is not rest the best therapy for extreme tiredness? If your advice implies that the patient is not as tired as he pretends, for example, in suggesting that he engage in more pleasant activities, your advice will not fit his goal of treating real fatigue. Hence, the patient will reject this advice, thus proving to be less tired than he pretends. This incongruent advice increases the probability that the patient will not comply with therapy.

Motivational strategies and reinforcement are core factors in childhood. Normally, crying babies motivate parents to feed and comfort the baby. On the other hand, too much crying creates irritation, sometimes resulting in neglect and aggression. Thus, attention seeking may motivate others to engage in or to avoid relationships. The motivational impact of behaviour is highly dependent on our current and past behavioural context. This context is supplied both verbally (pitch, intonation, tone and content of speech) and non-verbally (body language, eye contact and touch). We reinforce desired behaviours, but neglect, comment on or punish undesirable behaviour. Positive as well as negative attention and reactions are reinforcers. Punishment, reprimands and even physical violence may be perceived as reinforcers, as will certainly be the case in individuals with a history of neglect. Although such acts may be unethical, science applies the technical term 'positive reinforcement'. Reinforcement may be given consciously and explicitly, unconsciously and implicitly, and directly or indirectly.

Context may serve as a reinforcer too. For example, we create a positive atmosphere with flowers, music, food or mood lighting. It is wise to take the preferences of the receiver into account when selecting reinforcers. Most of the time, musical reinforcers that are most pleasing to 'hard metal' fans will be repulsive for opera lovers! Western women will appreciate a bouquet of flowers, but cut flowers, particularly white ones, are offensive in other cultures because they refer to death. Greeting people of the opposite sex with two kisses is normal in France, whereas three is usual in the Netherlands. However, Indians and Arabs do not kiss people of the opposite gender, and Inuits rub noses in greeting.

Motivation is about increasing advantages and reducing disadvantages. Manipulating a person's motivation is something of an art insofar as there is extreme diversity in humans as to what is and is not motivating. HIT applies the following motivation rules of thumb:

- Start imagining yourself in the other person's context. Study his or her habitual reaction patterns. Listen carefully and ask questions.
- Avoid conflicts.
- Socratic questioning is less risky than making statements or allegations.
- Maximize expectations about the ultimate goal.
- Split tasks into as many component steps as possible. Create subgoals. Introduce changes gradually, step by step.
- A multiple-choice or multi-option model decreases the risk of rejection.
- Be careful not to offer undesirable choices. All choices should lead to the final goal.

Increasing patients' motivation in health-care contexts requires deliberately and consistently increasing the readiness for change in patients and their systems. Motivation must be purposeful and goal-oriented. Goal-directed motivation involves proper knowledge of both the starting position and the final goal. It is risky to begin motivating someone before it has been determined whether patient, family and friends, and therapist are aiming at the same goal. A discrepancy in priorities between patient and therapist may alienate the patient from therapy. Instead, focus on creating an atmosphere of reliability and mutuality by inviting people to tell their stories. Lend them an empathetic ear, then explain your purpose and method, and finally ask them whether they agree to these.

Patients with chronic conditions and those with personality disorders run a relatively high risk of being disappointed in therapy. Start by asking your patients what they have already tried and to what effect. This will prevent the repetition of ineffective advice. It may also clear up their distrust, especially when you explicitly regret each disappointment. Be careful not to disrespect former therapists; regretting failures will do. Praise patients with chronic conditions for their endurance and their courage to continue asking for help. They will certainly appreciate this. In most cases, a little exaggeration is more effective than a compact attitude. It may cost some time, but the benefit is that people feel heard. As a result of this approach patients become more open. They will talk about former disappointments, about factors that have obstructed and may still obstruct or positively influence their health. Factors that with proper use may deliver opportunities for change or may be useful in the process of recovery.

The aforementioned two groups of patients easily induce negative expectations in therapists that may result in defensive attitudes. Asking patients to tell you what not to do based on their former experiences can be very effective. It helps both you and your patient. Your patients may cooperate by warning you whenever you are in danger of making the same errors as predecessor therapists.

If the advantages of a future state are more than the disadvantages of the present, people are normally motivated for change. Urgency, stage of treatment, patient's and therapist's personality characteristics, style of perception (in words, images or kinaesthetic), the system's characteristics and functionality of symptoms determine which motivational strategy is indicated.

Motivational strategies that are regularly used in HIT

The following strategies will be discussed: styles of communication, generating hope, the customer is always right, framing and positive reframing and labelling, Socratic questioning, refocusing on strengths and successes, taking advantage of personality traits, translating complaints into goals, selective reinforcement and operant conditioning, motivational interviewing, mental judo and aikido techniques, hypercongruent reactions, and attuning to the preferred style of perception.

Styles of communication

Communication is an interactive process. It is impossible not to communicate. A message may be communicated verbally, non-verbally and with silence. People make use of three different communication styles: symmetrical, complementary and parallel. Recognizing and adapting to somebody's preferred style prevents trouble.

When two people react similarly in a therapeutic context it is termed symmetry. When symmetry goes too far, an escalating argument may occur. The argument stops when one party stops. Most often this does not last. In cases of extreme symmetry, a new round of escalation is to be expected. Symmetrical challenges to paranoid delusions do not work for two reasons. First, by definition, a delusion is extremely resistant to change by others if at all. Second, the paranoid person may feel offended and sever contact. The patient may interpret courteous and friendly behaviour as 'proof' of the therapist's unreliability: the deluded conclusion being that you are attempting to tease a secret from him or her under false pretences. A more objective style of communication is advisable with paranoid patients.

Complementary communication is when one side speaks and the other listens. Examples of complementary relationships are sick–healthy, active–passive, spontaneous–reactive, extravert–introvert, gloomy–cheerful, and relationships between disabled and healthy individuals. Disabilities due to (psychiatric) disorders are common, and imply dependency on others to some extent in some domain for some time. This dynamic interaction reinforces relatives and therapists for behaving dominantly towards patients and people with disabilities. Hence, disabilities induce complementary relationships between patients, relatives and therapists. Complementarity tends to increase through the years. The complementary style is not the same as an authoritarian attitude.

Parallel relationships alternate between symmetrical and complementary communication styles depending on subject and context. Parallel communication offers the best opportunity for flexible adjustment to changing circumstances.

At the beginning of therapy, symmetrical communication with open-ended questions and an invitational attitude is the preferred style. In the current style of treatment the therapeutic relationship tends towards complementarity. The therapist starts posing targeted questions, interprets data and gives advice based on his or her expertise. Ideally, communication becomes parallel over time. However, chronicity requires a continuity of care that may necessitate a long-term complementary relationship.

Human communication has both a content and a process level. The content of a communication is what is being said, while the process side gives the deeper meaning, message or context. The context determines the relationship between people. It is a meta-message, a message about the message. For example, in traffic, the order 'Stop!' has more effect when given by a policeman than by a therapist. The uniform makes the difference. It gives status, or power, and power gives impact to words. Whether a message is understood depends to a great degree on its process level. A person's aura, his or her image, framing and the process of messages sometimes have more impact than their content. Expectations, sympathy with the message and the messenger are important. Expectations are not static. They can be moulded. Film scores are a good example: pace, instrumentation, timbre and tempo prepare us for the coming event as well as its emotional loading. The music induces emotional expectations. Similarly, expressions such as 'When you . . . ' or 'In time, . . . ' prepare the listener for future changes. Gift-wrapping raises expectations about the content of a box. Presentation has suggestive power. Our behaviour has this power too. A grave voice suggests mysteriousness or a threat. The sound 'ohh' may suggest more gloominess than 'ahh'. A tall chair gives a dominant position; someone wearing a three-piece suit elicits expectations different from those given by someone in jeans. These expectations depend on the context: are we in a bank or a disco?

Implicit and explicit rules govern communication. These rules mutually affect each other in a circular process that determines human behaviour and relationships. Behaviour affects the nature of relationships, which in turn affects the system of implicit and explicit rules (Watzlawick *et al.*, 1967). Western culture and language make use of linear cause–effect connections created by interpretation. Is someone silent because another person is speaking too much, or is the latter person talking so much because he or she has to fill the gaps left by the silent person? The interpretation of the silence is determined by the punctuation of the communication pattern, or the interpreted beginnings and ends of communication. Punctuation marks the beginning (attributions of guilt) and end (reaction of the victim) of sequences. Problems of punctuation are normal in conflicts. Dutch history books blame the English for starting wars in the seventeenth century, but English books blame the Dutch for this war. Saddam Hussein blamed America for interference in internal affairs, while the USA claimed the invasion of Iraq was to liberate the people from a dictator. Republicans blame Democrats and vice versa for the economic crisis. Both parties claim they are right.

Punctuation can be used to defend one party and to offend the other. This may happen unintentionally and unconsciously, with destructive reproaches and unnecessary references to the past. Impasses appear and communication patterns become chronic from the moment that one side expects the other to make the first move towards change. For example, a woman may say that she wants her husband to talk more and be open, while the man says that he wants his wife to stop carping and nagging. Parties keep each other in confinement, the indicated intervention is to replace 'if – then' with 'and – and'.

Generating hope

Hope keeps us alive. It may be increased in several ways and to varying degrees. The same statement can be made with varying degrees of implied hopefulness. The statement '70% of patients are benefitted by this treatment' is as right as the statement that 'it doesn't help 30%'. But the first statement evokes more hope than the latter. This kind of reframing may be used in clinical practise. You may explain that the disadvantage of drugs is their side-effects and tell the patient to call you immediately if any appear. This is a frightening message that may stress patients and make them hypervigilant towards side-effects. Why not go with the alternative: 'Side-effects are normal signals of the drug's effect. They mean that your prescription is working. Call me when you notice them so we can decide whether your dosage needs adjustment?' Be honest. Do not fake, regardless of your style. Prevention is better than cure.

Therapists may increase hope by showing expertise. Some hang diplomas on the wall. This may work in Asia or in the USA, but certainly not in Europe where this can be thought to be boastful. Hope may be shown more indirectly as well. For example, mentioning former therapeutic successes suggests expertise and generates hope. Therapists with less experience may refer to scientific literature or to the successes of their colleagues with the indicated treatment. Person-tailored psychoeducation also shows your expertise. And questions such as 'Many of my patients suffer from . . . how about you?' illustrate commitment, expertise and create expectations about your experience.

The customer is always right

Most patients prefer a positive approach. They react to positive interactions more cooperatively and compliantly than to interactions they experience as negative (Cohen and Berk, 1985). For this reason, it is better to avoid explaining treatment resistance in typical psychiatric language (van Os *et al.*, 2005). It is better to reframe resistance as a client's complaint because the latter term suggests the need for negotiation and resolution. We have found very positive results with relabelling objections against medication as requests for adjustment. This is perhaps unsurprising, as it is known that a permissive, negotiation-oriented style of communication combined with positive reframing leads to fewer conflicts and more win–win situations (Table 4.2).

Positive reframing

Before reading this item please answer the following question: how many numbers 9 do you count between 0 and 100? Start with 9, 19, 29 and so on. How many did you count? You probably have counted 10 or 11. However, the correct answer is 19. How could this happen? The examples given have framed your thoughts, ripening you for unconsciously ignoring 91, 92, etc. This is called framing. Framing steers your process of thinking, focuses your attention and may induce selective ignorance.

HIT promotes empowerment by reinforcing successes and patients' positive aspects. Positive reframing is probably the strongest motivational intervention. Any behaviour, complaint, sign and symptom allows for positive labelling, though positive reframing requires attention for the right moment of application. Positive reframing differs from complimenting: the former is change-oriented and offers new interpretations of events, experiences and behaviours that are different

Table 4.2 Fighting, negotiating and cooperation

Fighting	Negotiating	Cooperation
At least one loser	Partial win–win	No losers
Search for guilty subjects	Search for partial acceptable loss	Search for a common goal
Negative emotion directed	Goal directed	Positive emotion and goal directed
No opponent-directed listening	Wish-directed listening	Task-directed listening
Pseudo-questioning	Getting concrete the wishes of opponents	Making concrete goals and division of labour

from (the patient's) habitual interpretations. The method is applicable irrespective of circumstances, personality trait or disorder. Certain words and phrases consistently raise trust and readiness for cooperation, while other words easily raise resistance. A useful exercise is to construct a list of positive labels for common complaints and symptoms, especially for resistance, rejection and negativism that we sometimes encounter in daily practice. For example, a quiet person probably prefers the phrase 'still waters run deep' to being called 'boring'. 'He is a good listener' evokes more goodwill than 'he never says a word'. People prefer being called modest to being called shy or weird.

Positive labels may produce negative effects on a systems level too. A patient's friends or family may interpret destigmatizing reframed comments about the patient as accusations intended for them. Relabelling and re-attribution demand delicacy, especially in patients with chronic disorders. Parents will not be thankful for an explanation that their child's apathy is highly dependent upon their own overly dominant behaviour. Drop-out is a more probable reaction. Certainly, no dominant parent will appreciate the label 'dominant'. Neither do they deserve it, as they are trying to do their utmost. In lieu of confrontation – which is ineffective in decreasing resistance – I ask parents to help me by just closely observing their child's natural behaviour (which they already do, but now with an indirect order of not interfering). This may provide the therapist with the necessary information, and will also interfere with dominant parental behaviour while allowing the parent to save face.

Other kinds of reframing may be less offensive and more effective. Parental behaviour is likely to improve if parents prove open to the suggestion that their apathetic child may be a silent thinker who would rather bite his tongue than talk nonsense. Always be careful not to proffer certainties, or statements such as 'You are not apathetic, you are a thinker-type'. Instead, start by asking, 'Do you have impulsive inclinations? Do you act thoughtlessly?' The apathetic child will not be able to answer these question affirmatively. Hence, we can react with, 'I thought so, in my mind you are more a thinker-type'. This conclusion wipes away the apathetic label without openly confronting the parents.

Not all behaviour can be addressed with positive labelling. How can one reframe assault, incest and other forms of violence positively without invalidating the victim? It is a legitimate ethical question to ask how one can balance the rights, health and privacy of victims with an understanding of the intrapsychic and interpersonal conflicts that may have contributed to the behaviour of the perpetrator.

Socratic questioning

The Socratic method allows the therapist to refrain from giving direct advice. His or her focus is not on demonstrating that the therapist is right and the patient is wrong. Instead, the therapist attempts to evoke the development of the patient's own ideas for change and alternative solutions. The therapist may 'tempt' the patient into doubting by applying an indirect style of questioning of maladaptive thoughts. HIT values questions more than statements. Hence, the former are the preferred form of communication. Examples of questions include: 'Could it be possible that . . . ? Did you know . . . ? What do you think of . . . ?' instead of 'It has been proven that . . . It certainly is so-and-so . . . ' and so on. Socratic reasoning rarely results in conflicts. When a patient rejects or reacts negatively to a proposal phrased as 'What would you think if I proposed you to try . . . ?', the therapist can switch to another proposal without losing face. In contrast, the proposal, 'I suggest that you . . . ' leaves little room for a subject's change without losing face. Assignments posed in terms of do's and don't's, or phrases such as 'you have to . . . ' are evoking conflict.

Refocusing on strengths and successes

The more severe a symptom, the more it becomes the centre of attention and vice versa. The more attention symptoms attract, the more we become self-conscious and worry about them. If this continues, it becomes increasingly difficult to divert our attention to positive behaviours, skills and traits.

Assessing the strengths and successes of a patient has diagnostic as well as therapeutic value. Diagnostically, it tells us to what degree symptoms monopolize the life of the patient, and about the patient's relative centration on his or her disabilities. The more a patient's attention can be therapeutically diverted to other subjects or objects, the better the chances of improvement. Asking about successes may raise hope, but can also focus patients more on their problems, and make them feel ignored or misunderstood. Some patients may interpret our questions about delusions as proof that we do not believe them, or see them as poseurs. Reframing and positive labelling are useful here.

Taking advantage of personality traits

People with cluster A personality traits are unusually suspicious and distant. They are self-contained and introverted, do not attach much value to intimacy, and react rather coldly to others. For them, empathy, including therapeutic empathy, may feel uncomfortable. With these patients, a more distant, neutral attitude is recommended. Sitting at a table often works well because it both creates some physical distance and suggests a working atmosphere.

For people with cluster B personalities a more personal style is indicated. Cluster B personality types have ambivalence (hold me and leave me) and commonly fear responsibility for their decisions and behaviour. Therefore, direct advice amenable to one exclusive explanation is best avoided. Unequivocal suggestions unavoidably fulfil one side of an ambivalent person's contradictory desires. Such advice is lacking. A dialectical approach better serves their ambivalence. One may try: 'Normally I suggest doing X, but in view of your experiences Y may be better'. I have good results with the following sentences: 'Two different forces in you are fighting for victory, and you are the victim. Until we fully understand this conflict, both sides need gratification. Please close your right mental ear and I'll counsel force one. Next, close your other mental ear and I'll counsel force two'. Although this may sound odd to someone without cluster B, many people with a cluster B personality structure recognize this distinction within themselves. Do not put too much emphasis on their obligation for self-determination and responsibility. Due to a fear of being held responsible for their behaviour this may elicit their resistance. A permissive style that offers suggestions through Socratic questioning is preferable.

People with a narcissistic personality disorder will not take orders. By definition, they know better and need to make decisions on their own. The stronger these traits, the greater their aversion to perceived slights to their autonomy. For them, multiple-choice advice is better than prescriptions. Have them choose between at least two options. Negotiate on which drug suits them better. Do they prefer a long-lasting drug or more doses per day? Ask about the best time for observation of and monitoring their symptoms, accept their preference and tempo. But regret openly that observation for only one hour a day may delay the start of treatment. Another option is to capitalize on their narcissism by doubting whether they will be able to perform a task. They will usually accept the challenge and attempt to prove you are wrong.

Shy and social phobic persons (cluster C traits) experience difficulties in making decisions. Either–or choices are off-putting. Unlike people with cluster B traits, they need solidity, structure and guidance, as do autistic and intellectually disabled patients. Negotiations may last several therapeutic sessions. Either–or choices may be replaced by 'and–and' tasks, or 'on–off' homework: one week task A, the next week task B. In completing these assignments, patients examine which task suits them best and which homework has the best effect.

Let me make some remarks on observation. (1) Symptom observation is intended to provide information. As soon as the desired information has been collected, further monitoring of symptoms is meaningless. (2) Monitoring of effect requires the patient (and key figures) to monitor his or her coping and its effect. This type of monitoring may provide information about compliance too. (3) Stop monitoring as soon as this becomes part of obsessive behaviour.

Changing the agenda: translating complaints into targets

With this method the therapist orients discussions towards actions (e.g. by reframing complaints and symptoms into steps to be taken by the patient), and reinforcing compliance through operant conditioning.

The first step of therapy should be a detailed survey of symptoms, complaints, emotions, thoughts and behaviour. Because most mental health patients are suffering, this information is usually negative, which makes it difficult to raise hope during the diagnostic stage. Empathetic affective reflections such as: 'You feel depressed, desperate, powerless; you excessively worry, and are anxious' are common in clinical practice. However, these reflections may unintentionally increase the patient's despondency, especially when they are reiterated. The reflective statement: 'You can't get your life back on track and worrying is driving you crazy' may be factually right, but is counterproductive to restoring hope. The fact that the therapist seems to agree with the patient can magnify his or her feelings of inadequacy. In order to minimize these unwanted by-products of reflective listening, the therapist actively reframes symptoms as goals to achieve. For example, our earlier statement may have been better phrased as: 'You want to change the agenda, to get your life back on track and stop worrying. Am I right?' Instead of avoiding passive language, use active forms as much as possible. For example, reflect that a person is worrying (active) and not that he or she is getting overwhelmed (passive).

Next, translate symptoms into goals, brainstorm about possible solutions and choose one to start with. Make sure the plan of action is concrete. You might ask: Who will take which actions at which moment? How much time will you spend on this? Who is going to assist you? And finally: Which obstacles might interfere with the performance? What can you do to prevent this or to tackle unexpected obstacles?

Selective operant conditioning

Success motivates future successes. It also indirectly reinforces therapy adherence and any effort expended. Successes invite friends and family to provide positive reinforcement. Small assignments are therefore better reinforcers than bigger tasks because success and hence reinforcement is delayed in the latter. Split assignments into smaller, easier chunks (as many as possible) so that failure is nearly impossible. In this way, each piece becomes an opportunity for success. Chunking increases the frequency of reinforcement through success, and reduces chances of failure.

Selective operant conditioning helps to strengthen low self-esteem and ailing ego functions. Recalling successes is better for damaged self-confidence than repeating failures. Patients with negative self-image are used to emphasizing the negative. Some insight-oriented therapies emphasize the value of re-experiencing negative memories in detail. These therapies usually take years. An interesting alternative is to dwell on a person's successes and enquire explicitly about moments when he or she overcame barriers and tackled setbacks. Examine the differences in thoughts and feelings that accompany failure and success. Self-monitoring may help patients.

A focus on success requires a proactive approach from therapists. The therapist needs to be vigilant for opportunities to reinforce successes and to find them in the first place. For example, when a patient tells you that a homework assignment did not work, you may respond with an opportunity for positive reframing: 'What a pity. How did you do it?' If the patient did not try, a negative effect is to be expected. Suggest a second adjusted try. If the patient tried but was unsuccessful, your reactions will centre around 'great perseverance!' Then, in reviewing the patient's self-monitoring exercises, you might notice that scores after performing the task were actually better than before having done the task. Your next question could be: 'Do you mind if we go over your self-monitoring homework?' Do not simply accept failures; analyse them and frame them as opportunities for future success. After scrutinizing the scores, the patient may agree that the homework had some effect, but he or she is dissatisfied with its degree of efficacy and duration. Three choices present themselves:

- You emphatically agree with your patient's disappointment. The advantage of this approach is that the patient feels understood. Disadvantages include: reinforcement of their disability, weakening their trust in your therapy for the homework was ineffective, and the need to choose another approach that is likely to fail as well.
- You point out improvements in contrast with past failures: 'For how long have you had this symptom? Three years? So, for all those years you have tried your best, but unfortunately without success. More than that, your symptoms became worse. Do you realize that this is the first moment of some improvement? You are being pretty modest about your success. Do you want to try for further improvement?'
- You focus on success. 'Okay, you aren't satisfied with a one point reduction in your misery [imagine a reduction in misery from 7 to 6]. Tell me, when you're shopping, do you prefer paying full price or a 10% discount? You like the discount? Can you explain why a person would appreciate a 10% discount, but not appreciate a 15% reduction in suffering?' The patient's reactions are purposely evoked because they give elbow-room for shifts in the flow of therapy.

Operant conditioning may also be used to minimize drop-out and treatment non-compliance. One of the ways operant conditioning is used in HIT is by adjusting the interval time between sessions. In most treatment paradigms, the time between sessions is shortened when problems arise, deterioration occurs or improvements fail to occur. In contrast, HIT therapists are more likely to extend the interval between sessions when patients do not comply with homework, resist treatment or appear to be in danger of overextending themselves. This extension might seem harsh at first. However, behavioural theory and our clinical experience suggest that it is good for some patients. Decreasing the interval between sessions when patients have trouble with therapy means rushing the very patients who need more time to fulfil therapeutic tasks. These patients deserve extra time between sessions instead. For patients with difficulties following therapeutic advice, each session means repeating excuses for being unable to perform again and again. Their self-esteem will not improve through this repetitive confrontation with their disability. Their failures may result in resistance. We refrain from seeing patients more frequently when they are struggling because this may reinforce low self-esteem.

Another problem with shortening the inter-session interval is that patients are likely to miss sessions repeatedly. Their difficulty observing appointments will have to be addressed as possible avoidance.

   Allotting too much time to these 'difficulties' is usually a trap. The behaviour is symptomatic: talking about a task in lieu of doing it (avoidance). It is my experience that in such cases lengthening the inter-session interval may have miraculous powers. The method is as follows: The 'pathological' avoidance behaviour is relabelled positively as 'not yet getting around to finishing the task' or 'paying attention to your energy level' and requiring more time. The therapist grants the desired increase in inter-session time while promising to meet with the patient earlier just in case he or she is able to complete the task earlier. (Be wary of countertransference. Increasing inter-session time should never be used as punishment.) Most avoidant patients end up calling for an early appointment, especially those who generally appreciate the therapeutic contact with you. Of course, this intervention approach is contraindicated in cases of true emergency and suicide attempts.

Motivational interviewing

Prochaska and DiClemente (1982) distinguished between six stages in a cyclic process of change. Each successive stage represents an increasing degree of readiness for change. Figure 4.1 illustrates these stages. Each stage has specific characteristics that require stage-specific motivational strategies.

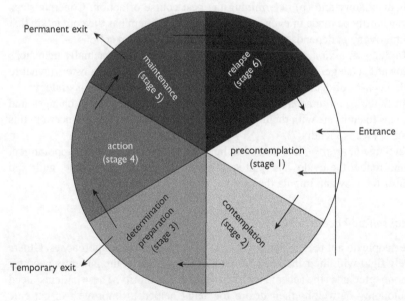

UNRAB – University of Nijmegen Research Group on Addictive Behaviour

Figure 4.1 A stage model of the process of change. Adapted from Prochaska *et al.* (1992).

Patients are insufficiently ready to implement change before Stage 4. Premature suggestions to take medication and make lifestyle changes potentially threaten the therapeutic alliance and increase risks of non-compliance and drop-out.

Miller and Rolnick (1991) have translated this transdiagnostic theory of change into concrete motivational strategies:

- In Stage 1, *precontemplation*, the person does not recognize or ignores that there is a problem that needs change. Recommended interventions involve provoking doubt and improving the patient's cognizance of risks of and problems with current behaviour. Helpful strategies at this stage include empathetic questioning and reflective summarizing of suffering. The greater the gap you can create between the patient's perceptions of their present state and their goals the better. Do not emphasize possible successes of change too much at this stage. I prefer comments like, 'I wouldn't hold it against you if you weren't as successful at this as patient X'.
- In Stage 2, *contemplation*, some doubts have already been formed. Tipping the balance towards a desire for change is pivotal at this stage. The therapist evokes reasons for change, hints at the risks of not changing and strengthens the patient's self-efficacy for change.
- In Stage 3, *determination*, the patient has decided that something has to be done. However, the patient needs help in (a) deciding that his or her action is mandatory and (b) determining the best course of action. Concrete steps can hardly be made or even planned before the patient has the conviction that improvement depends to some extent on his or her own actions.
- In Stage 4, *action*, you can focus on helping the patient actually take steps towards change. The more concrete the steps the better. Brainstorm what to do in cases of disappointment or failure with the chosen coping strategy.
- In Stage 5, *maintenance*, the patient has made the necessary changes and plans to continue with them. Relapse prevention is the central concern in this stage (see Appendix 7).
- In Stage 6, *relapse*, it is crucial to help the patient overcome disappointment and renew the cycle. The patient must tackle feelings of shame, guilt and insufficiency and initiate the cycle of change once more.

Mental self-defence techniques

Some people do not feel helped by straightforward, congruent approaches. Others actively fight with their therapist for power. Occasionally, the patient's need for autonomy precludes the acceptance of professional authority. These patients' need for autonomy outweighs their desire for being helped to improve. An extreme example can be found in patients with a narcissistic or a passive-aggressive personality structure, who may constantly resist demands for social participation and effort (American Psychiatric Association, 1994). The patients dawdle, become stubborn, or irritated when they have to do things they do not like. They may avoid obligations on the pretext of forgetfulness or that they doubt the value of therapist and approach. This resistance to change and recovery is systemic. It requires a non-congruent approach.

Mental judo and aikido are special methods of going along with resistance in order to take over (Lange, 1985). The therapist avoids 'pulling' the patient in a certain direction and refrains from offering positive comments or hopeful conclusions. The therapist may be more likely to label complaints and symptoms as severe and difficult to treat, express his or her hope for the best outcome, but take a gloomy view on the possibilities for change. A modest position is chosen. Right after suggesting an idea the therapist withdraws it, because: 'I don't want to lead you along'. He or she may put forward considerations but, on second thoughts, doubt their efficacy in *this* patient. The therapist's suggestions are indirect and hidden. At the same time, he or she generates hope by telling of successful treatments in other patients. The therapist expresses a desire for similar results with the current patient, but wonders aloud whether this is realistic. The therapist steers communication, and when a patient requests whether they should take medication A, or use technique B, he or she leaves it open: 'I understand what you want to do. You can try, I hope it will help, but I can't give you any guarantee'.

Choosing between judo/aikido and congruent approaches is not easy. Some indicators may help you in deciding which one to use: The 'yes-but patient' views arguments and suggestions positively. Unfortunately, there are always reasons and circumstances that prevent their implementation or make them inapplicable. A congruent relationship may backfire here. These patients test the therapist, who will have increasing difficulty coming up with new solutions and suggestions that cannot withstand the persistent criticism. Some variants on the typical 'yes-but' response are 'This is who I am', 'It's in the family', 'That doesn't fit my personality', 'I'm afraid I'm too sensitive for that', etc. These patients rarely reject the therapist's advice openly. They may fully endorse it. Unfortunately, it does not fit them.

The following characteristics can be found in these patients: strong assertiveness, chronic functional symptoms, prior failures of congruent therapies, symptomatic behaviour, difficulty de-escalating or refraining from power struggles.

Standard solutions for this 'yes-but' pattern do not exist, but the following approaches may be effective:

- Adopt the 'yes-but' pattern. Report extensively on similar, but not identical cases that were successfully treated using x, y or z. Follow these stories along the lines of, 'What a pity that this kind of therapy is highly idiosyncratic. Otherwise, I would certainly suggest a similar treatment for you.' Or, 'Excuse me for bothering you. I get too enthusiastic sometimes. But you're right, someone else's success isn't your affair.'
- Propose two approaches to doubtful patients and have them examine which approach suits them best by monitoring their effects. If they still hesitate, let them throw a dice to decide which approach to start with.

- Give contrarian patients good advice that you withdraw on second thoughts for reasons that it is possibly inadequate for them. Replace the withdrawn proposal with a more difficult (but as effective) proposal. The second proposal makes the first one appear more attractive in contrast. Quite a few of my patients tried the withdrawn proposal. The slight provocation of narcissistic patients as mentioned before may help here.
- Respond to competitive behaviour and pride by postponing an intervention because the patient probably is not yet ready for it.
- Suggest to a patient that they imagine a symptom-free day. Unconscious fears, resistance, barriers and frustrating consequences of improvement may become clear. Target obstacles to change following the Miller and Rolnick's stages. Finally, ask the patient to fill the gaps left by the disappeared symptom *before* considering improvement.

Hypercongruent interventions

Giving advice only to withdraw it is an example of a hypercongruent intervention. The main indicators for hypercongruent interventions are: resistance to or ineffectiveness of congruent strategies and medication. Both these forms of treatment resistance are common by-products of delusions and hallucinations. As described above, treatment resistance may also be found in patients with personality disorders (especially cluster B). The combination of severe ambivalence and fear of assault on their autonomy requires a double-barrelled therapy. Building a hypercongruent intervention means: (1) simultaneously endorsing opposing poles and (2) simultaneously working towards both poles individually with specific pole-oriented suggestions that may be in mutual conflict. For example: I may advise the patient to get sufficient rest (pole 1) and also to vent his aggression through activity (pole 2). Whatever the patient's behaviour, he cannot do anything but cooperate. Either he has vented in agreement with my advice for pole 2, or he has not, which may be described as getting rest in agreement with pole 1.

Of course, patients may ask you what specific behaviours they should perform. To my surprise, replying, 'Just do what you/your unconscious know is best' appears to be a satisfactory answer for most patients.

Adjusting to the patient's perceptive style

The therapist should anticipate and join in with the patient's preferred perceptive style, whether visual, verbal or kinaesthetic. People who prefer getting information verbally prefer speech. Those who have a visual perceptive style prefer leaflets and the internet, using images and colours. These people *see* their future, prefer video or text to verbal and audio information. Verbally oriented people are more talkative. They prefer the spoken word. Facts *speak for* themselves. A visually oriented person may not have *seen* someone lately, a verbal person has not *spoken* to them. A kinaesthetic preference may be humoured with such sentences as: the rumour *goes*, my reputation has *gone*, I am *doing* badly. If a kinaesthetic person is depressed, then the walls are closing in on him or her, while the visual person sees a dark future. Communication with patients in their preferred style is recommended.

Material motivation

In addition to psychosocial motivational interventions, material rewards may have motivating effects too. These reinforcers can tip the scale towards compliance and cooperation. However, their effectiveness is contextually and socially dependent. In the Netherlands with good national social insurance systems and sickness funds, patients take free medication and meals for granted. Institutions in the USA, on the other hand, may be able to use these inducements as a reward for compliance.

Diagnosing auditory verbal hallucinations

There is no strict distinction between the diagnostic and therapeutic stages in HIT. Its way of questioning includes elements of both. The diagnostic process concerns:

- somatic disorders and side-effects of medication;
- psychiatric disorders;
- the impact of relationships and of the patient's personality;
- characteristics of the voices (AVHRS: Jenner and van de Willige, 2002, Appendix 1; Positive and Useful Voices Inventory: Jenner *et al.*, 2008, Appendix 2), including their supposed meaning and causes;
- 'functionality' and 'secondary gain' of voice hearing;
- patterns of selective reinforcement;
- coping repertoire (Coping with Voices Inventory: Jenner and Geelhoed-Jenner, 1998, Appendix 3);
- readiness for change (illness-awareness cycle of Prochaska and DiClemente, 1982); and
- inability or unwillingness.

A thorough physical examination to rule out somatic disorders and side-effects of medication must precede treatment. Nearly all medications can cause hallucinations, even antidepressants and antipsychotics. Deafness and cerebral disorders may cause musical hallucinations in non-psychotic patients. Secondary deafness is strongly associated with AVH in the deaf ear and also with paranoia (Almeida *et al.*, 1993; Berrios, 1990). In prelingual deaf patients, visual and tactile hallucinations are more common than AVH, although voice hearing has been reported in these patients as well (Schonauer *et al.*, 1998).

Most psychiatric patients are clearly conscious when they hallucinate. Exceptions include narrowing of attention during dissociative periods, and broadening during intoxication. Practitioners must also be attentive to delirium, which can be easily missed due to temporary states of clear consciousness. Clinical observation of patients with delirium is mandatory for proper diagnosis as well as risk management.

HIT's '11 step' diagnostic procedure

Studies have demonstrated that hallucinations are easily missed even by experienced therapists. Voice hearers are reluctant to report their voices, and therapists do not always probe for them sufficiently. In one study of hallucination in childhood only 30% of parents knew that their child heard AVHs (Bartels-Velthuis *et al.*, 2010).

The diagnostic process starts with a differential diagnosis differentiating AVH from look-a-like symptoms. Next, assessment of AVHs should include: (a) are the patient's experiences perceptions, (b) are the perceptions hallucinations; and (c) are the hallucinations abnormal? If these questions are answered in the affirmative, the clinician should determine whether the cause of the hallucinations is somatic, psychological or due to medication. Therapeutically important issues – personality traits and habitual patterns of behaviour – need to be assessed as well. It is advisable to follow a diagnostic protocol. The following stepwise diagnostic protocol (Table 4.3) can help to optimize hallucination diagnosis (Jenner, 2012a, 2012b).

Step 1: Differential diagnosis

In many cases, the phenomenology of AVH differs little from hearing actual voices. Over 70% of voice hearers report that AVH volumes are comparable to normal conversation (Nayani and David, 1996). The phenomenology of AVH does not differ much across psychiatric disorders. That of patients diagnosed with schizophrenia is strikingly similar to that of patients with borderline personality disorder, including their perceived location, malevolence, duration, loudness, and even subjects' beliefs about their origin (Hepworth *et al.*, 2013). These points notwithstanding, phenomenology is a crucial diagnostic parameter for AVH. The distinction from obsessive–compulsive thoughts may be difficult in the case of overwhelming emotions and delusions.

Diagnostically, hallucinations need to be differentiated from dreams, pseudohallucinations, illusions and obsessive–compulsive thoughts. This differentiation has implications for treatment. In all cases, alert consciousness is mandatory in AVH.

- *Dreams*: A dream is an altered state of consciousness that occurs during sleep, in contrast to hallucinations which occur during wakefulness. One might compare daydreaming to hallucinations or hypothesize that these are a special type of hallucination.
- *Pseudohallucinations*: The word pseudohallucination has historically been defined in two distinct ways. According to the first definition, pseudohallucinations are voices that a person experiences as coming from inside his

Table 4.3 HIT protocol for assessing AVHs

Step	Assessment objective	Tool	Comment
1	Differential diagnosis	Psychiatric interview	Discriminate: hallucinations, dreams and OCD
2	AVH?	Validate physical qualities	Physical qualities differentiates AVH from: illusion, delusion and obsessive–compulsive thought
3	(mortal) Danger?	Psychiatric interview and testing (PANSS etc.)	Most hallucinations have low mortal risk, except those with aforementioned characteristics • Obedience to voices • Command hallucination • Delusions of being controlled, paranoia or reference
4	Somatic disorders?	Anamnesis and physical examination	Treatment focus on: • somatic diseases • medication side-effects
5	Psychiatric disorder?	Psychiatric interview	Use guidelines
6	Habitual reaction pattern, personality traits?	Psychiatric interview and psychological testing	Indicate the preferred style of communication
7	AVH characteristics?	AVHRS and PUVI	Necessary for fine-tuning of treatment programme
8	Selective reinforcement?	Functional analysis	Necessary for fine-tuning of treatment programme
9	Functionality and secondary gain?	CVI	Necessary for fine-tuning of treatment programme
10	Habitual patient's and relatives' behaviour patterns?	Interaction analysis and systems assessment	Necessary for fine-tuning of treatment programme
11	Willingness and disability vs. reluctance?	In-depth interview	Necessary for fine-tuning of treatment programme

or her head. According to the second definition, pseudohallucination is a label used to describe the experience of voice hearers who know that their AVHs are not real perceptions. Following this definition, hypnagogic and hypnopompic hallucinations, visual hallucinations of the Charles Bonnet syndrome and migraine auras are pseudohallucinations. Subjects with true hallucinations lack this awareness. Many authors have cast doubt on the theoretical validity of distinguishing between hallucinations and pseudohallucinations. Studies comparing AVHs associated with borderline personality disorder – historically defined as pseudohallucinations – and AVH with schizophrenia, have failed to provide empirical justification for the label (Slotema and Kingdon, 2012). Speaking about pseudohallucinations in general, Berrios wrote: 'It can be concluded that pseudohallucination is a vicarious construct (i.e. one created by a contemporary conceptual need, and which is not associated with a biological invariant and that it is used as the "Joker" in a poker game. . . .). Therefore, it looks as if the concept is irretrievably fuzzy and needs to be abandoned' (p. 60). In their review, Van der Zwaard and Polak (1999) explain how the value of the distinction between hallucination and pseudohallucination is increasingly doubted in the scientific arena.

- *Imaginations*: Unlike hallucination, imagination lacks a compelling sense of reality, and is more amenable to control.
- *Illusions*: Illusions are misinterpretations of real, external and perceptible objects, such as a pine tree mistaken for a villain at dusk, or a ghost that in daylight proves to be a shirt. Illusions share with AVHs a similar sensory experience, but have a strong as-if quality. In an illusion an object seems to be there, and, at the same time, it is clear that it factually is not there. It is a kind of 'observation' with subtle indications of unreality. Illusions are the result of disturbances in imagery and misinterpretation. The more illusions resemble delusional thinking, the less correctable they are.
- *Obsessive–compulsive thinking*: Obsessive–compulsive thoughts lack sensory experience. However, the distinction with AVHs may be difficult in cases of overwhelming emotions or severe delusional aspects. Two aspects may complicate the distinction between AVH and obsessive–compulsive thoughts. First, the affective loading of obsessive–compulsive thoughts may have such intensity that they are experienced as spoken words. Second, disturbances in thinking similar to those found in obsessive–compulsive disorders frequently accompany hallucinations. Thus, AVHs may be missed. The fuzziness of the line between obsessive–compulsive thoughts and AVHs may also explain the effectiveness of 'thought stopping' in some voice hearers (Johnson *et al.*, 1983; Wolpe, 1958).
- *Traumatic events*: The reliving of traumatic events often featured in PTSD can usually be differentiated from hallucinations. Patients with PTSD realize that their experiences represent memories. In cases of overwhelming experience the line may blur, but will reinstate itself in due time.

Apparently, idiosyncratic, strange experiences such as hallucinations can induce idiosyncratic, incorrigible thought processes. It is advisable to continually inquire into the sensory quality and reality of perceptions. You may ask questions such as: Do you hear the voice similarly to how you hear mine? Does it sound like a voice or *is* it a voice that you hear? In what way do you distinguish between a thought and the voice you hear? Do not forget to assess the imperative quality of voices. The more imperative and goal oriented the voice, the greater the risk of violence.

Step 2: Determine whether the voices are really heard

Are the voices experienced as sensory perceptions? In order to differentiate AVHs from illusions, delusions and obsessive–compulsive thoughts, ask the person about the physical qualities of their voices. AVHs may be experienced as external, coming from outside the head, and/or internal. Delirium can be ruled out if the patient is oriented to time, place and person.

Step 3: Assess risks

High risk is associated with compliance to command hallucinations, delusions of being controlled and of reference, and the content of paranoid delusions. Most of the time, AVHs in psychiatric patients have a negative, nasty content. Voices may command the patient to oppose treatment and neglect their own health. Less frequent but more dangerous voices command the patient to self-mutilate, commit suicide or homicide. In the case of command hallucinations, the danger depends in part upon the degree of obedience to the voices and on compliance with treatment. While risk of most AVHs is low, consideration of these variables is important for ensuring safety. Really risky is the combination of AVHs + delusions, especially the paranoid, those of reference and of being controlled.

Step 4: Search for somatic disorders, as well as possible side-effects of medication

Somatic disorders and medication side-effects may cause AVHs. Consult the medical history and if possible perform a physical examination at intake. Hallucinations have been reported in nearly all somatic disorders, from fever, infection and dehydration to tumours, cardiovascular and metabolic diseases (e.g. diabetes, porphyria, thyroid pathology: Asaad and Shapiro, 1986). Rule out epilepsy and narcolepsy. Be aware that musical hallucinations commonly result from aural and cerebral illnesses. Visual hallucinations may result from delirium and substance intoxication.

Step 5: Assess for psychiatric disorders

Common psychiatric disorders associated with AVHs are dissociative identity disorder, schizophrenia spectrum disorder, PTSD, borderline personality disorder, psychotic depression and substance abuse. Apply the DSM-IV-TR or International Classification of Diseases (ICD-10) protocol or make use of specific diagnostic instruments such as the Positive and Negative Symptom Scale (PANSS), the Dissociation Questionnaire (DIS-Q) or Dissociation Experiences Scale (DES).

Step 6: Assess personality traits

This is important for two reasons. First, patients with schizotypal or borderline personality disorder frequently hear voices or have visions associated with their disorder. Second, habitual reaction patterns and personality traits of voice hearers and their relatives are indicative of the preferred style of communication. For example, while most people appreciate empathy, persons with schizotypal personalities prefer more distance. Paranoid persons may interpret our compassion as frightening proof that we can read their minds. Narcissistic individuals may have a grandiose sense of self-importance that prevents them from accepting even the best advice, and should therefore be given at least two effective optional suggestions or advices. Because patients with narcissistic personality disorder regularly reject (easy) homework, tasks should be presented as challenges, 'possibly too difficult' for the patient. Narcissistic patients will attempt to prove you are wrong.

Dialectical reasoning is a good approach for patients with borderline personality disorder. Many borderline patients appreciate it when their therapist endorses contradictory actions simultaneously (everyone is doing the best they can, *and* everyone needs to do better). They may want help, but experience help as frightening. Denying a request may be perceived as rejection and lead to conflict; however, giving help and holding them responsible for their behaviour are experienced as assaults on their autonomy. A dialectical approach that acknowledges both sides of an issue can help these patients learn to avoid black and white thinking and accept aid in an adaptive way.

Step 7: Assess the characteristics of AVHs

It is necessary to assess the characteristics of the hallucinations, their possible significance, and how patient and relatives explain the voices. Investigate their content, form and context. Are they negative, positive, neutral or useful? Do they predict, promise, comment, threaten or repeat? Which emotional loading do they exert? Do they have clear purposes? What meaning and attribution are the AVHs blamed for? Therapy compliance is an important reason for inquiry into positive and useful AVHs.

Various instruments are available for assessing AVHs. A comprehensive description of these can be found in Aleman and Larøi (2008). HIT applies the AVHRS (Jenner and van de Willige, 2002) and the Positive and Useful Voices Inventory (PUVI: Jenner et al., 2008). The AVHRS helps to assess specific AVH characteristics.

Content

Three types of AVH may be distinguished: negative, positive and useful ones. Two types of distinction are being made: the voice hearer's subjective value and the result of effectiveness. For example, a voice telling you that you have godly powers may be experienced positively, certainly by manic patients, but also negatively as demonic pride by some religious patients. The manic patient may value falsely his or her 'godly' voice as useful, which may result in civil commitment. For most subjects, their first AVHs have a negative content. However, positive AVHs are heard by 25–75% of subjects and useful ones by about 40% on a lifetime basis (Jenner *et al.*, 2008; Sanjuan *et al.*, 2004). About 25% of Spanish patients with schizophrenia reported positive AVHs, compared with 50% of Dutch patients. Members of the Dutch foundation 'Weerklank' (meaning echo or response) reported a 75% lifetime prevalence of positive AVHs.

Positive experienced AVHs give advice, help in performing daily activities and decision-making. Therapeutically, they can be effectively implemented against negative AVHs. Nevertheless, only about 32% of voice hearers want to preserve their positive AVHs. Useful voices may support the taking of medication, which some patients do not experience as positive, despite the positive effect of a 20% reduction in rehospitalization. Almost invariably, people who want to keep their positive AVHs have a real or at least perceived ability to control their AVHs. Positive AVHs tend to disappear over the years, but useful AVHs do not. Neither positive nor useful AVHs appeared to be significantly related to psychosis. However, non-psychotic voice hearers experience these types of AVHs more often than psychotic patients.

Contextual factors

Contextual factors relate to where and (since) when, triggers, interactions and the voice hearer's expectations. Whether there is a relationship between the AVHs and affective state is relevant, as are specific triggers.

Organization

How many voices are heard? Does the number and severity change over time? A direct relationship between severity and number of voices has been found (Bartels-Velthuis *et al.*, 2010). What is their gender? Do they speak in sequence? Does a hierarchy of voices exist and a relationship? Do they cooperate or fight? Do supporting AVHs exist?

Controlling the hallucinations

Is the voice hearer (in)dependent of the AVHs? Do they command or flatter? Can they be evoked? Is there communication with the AVHs? How do the AVHs react on coping behaviour such as negation, negotiation, threatening, ignoring, medication and cognitive techniques?

Who is in power – the voice hearer or their AVHs – and does the power balance switch depending on time or subject?

Familiarity

Does the voice hearer recognize the voice? Does the voice make itself known? If so, is he or she a person, a demon, a ghost, a devil, a god or a . . . ? Is it the voice of an acquaintance or authority? Does a relation with trauma exist?

Consequences

What changes have the AVHs organized in the voice hearer's life, in relationships, social contacts, work, etc.? What nasty things do AVHs make the voice hearer do? Which pleasant actions can he or she no longer perform? What are the consequences of these changes for the patient and his or her system?

Attributions of intent and purpose

Meaning and purpose of AVHs become clear by asking questions such as: Do you know why you hear voices, while others don't? Why are voices talking to you? What do they have in mind? What is their intention, are they good or aren't they? Do they intend to guide or protect you, or are they wholly terror or just a nuisance? Could they unknowingly be a part of your own self?

The AVHRS (Appendix 1) is a 16-item 5-point scale structured interview for assessing the number, content, frequency, duration, context, organization, location, degree of control, emotional experience, personal significance, explanation, and perceived impact of the voices. The reliability coefficient for the AVHRS based on 92 ratings from four raters was 0.84 (weighted kappa) and 0.71 for lifetime assessment. Internal consistency (Cronbach's alpha) was 0.84 in an adult sample and 0.77 in a sample of children. Pearson's correlation coefficients with Symptoms Checklist-90 were significant at $p < .01$ with depression, psychoticism, phobic anxiety and somatization and $p < .05$ with interpersonal sensitivity, anxiety, obsessive–compulsive symptoms and paranoid ideation ($r = 0.66$ with the psychoticism dimension). Agreement analyses showed weighted Cohen's kappa $= 0.84$. According to patients, face validity was very good (Bartels-Velthuis et al., 2012a).

Other instruments include the Psychotic Symptom Rating Scale (PSYRATS) subscales measuring hallucinations and delusions (Haddock et al., 1999). The AVH section of this self-report instrument consists of 11 items assessing dimensions of frequency, duration, location, beliefs, degree and amount of negative content, amount and intensity of distress, and the extent to which the voices disrupt the patient's life. The subscales have good interrater reliability.

The Auditory Hallucination Rating Scale (AHRS) developed by Hoffman *et al.* (2003) measures seven items: frequency, reality, loudness, number of voices, length, attentional salience and distress level. I am not aware of psychometric research of this scale.

Command hallucinations may be assessed with the Revised Beliefs About Voices Questionnaire (Chadwick *et al.*, 2000a). This 35-item self-report instrument (4-point scale) measures the person's perceptions and responses to AVH. It has five subscales measuring malevolence, benevolence, omnipotence, resistance and engagement.

Also, assessment of positive and useful voices is mandatory because non-compliance may result from patients' fear that these voices will disappear as undesirable side-effect of treatment. The PUVI (Appendix 2) is a 53-items self-report AVH inventory that assesses prevalence, course and characteristics of positive and useful AVH, and emotional attribution with two subscales exploring reasons for attributions. These subscales have good internal consistency (Cronbach's alpha: positive subscale = 0.92, useful scale = 0.89) and very good face validity (Jenner *et al.*, 2008).

Step 8: Determine to what extent the voices serve a function for the patient in terms of secondary gain

Is reciprocity present and are the hallucinations forms of symptomatic behaviour? Symptoms can act as non-verbal interpersonal messages that tell us: I am not responsible for my behaviour, nor am I to be blamed. It is my AVH, the conspiracy, my partner, society, my hereditary constitution, and so on that are at fault. Diagnosis and treatment have the potential to reinforce symptomatic behaviour. Drinkers may hide behind a genetic disorder, or their depression. Violent people may curse their troubled youth for being unable to change. Reinforcement may cause the symptoms to remain after its cause has long disappeared. It is important to search for exemption of duties that is given to voice hearers.

Step 9: Assess whether reactions from relatives selectively reinforce AVHs

Although symptoms do cause suffering and misery, they may also produce advantages for either the patient, his or her friends and family or both parties. Psychotic symptoms may help the patient to avoid intrapsychic conflicts, anxiety-provoking circumstances or difficult decisions. This is referred to as primary gain. Secondary gain stems from a desire for attention or exemption from an unpleasant task. The word gain is rather heart-rending because the 'gain' costs suffering and genuine symptoms. From a learning theory perspective, this gain does reinforce the impact of symptoms.

Case vignettes

John's voices have a peculiar pattern. Each time his brother gets a bigger steak his voices command him to steal the steak when saying prayers. Similarly, they command him to to take his brother's favourite cakes.

Mrs Pedroni's social phobia has got bizarre psychotic features. Ghosts threaten her with flying kitchen utensils. In a panic she calls her husband, who, being at work, calls their daughter to reassure her mother. The daughter calls her grandparents who come to reassure the mother. In this case all appeared to benefit. The patient's psychotic symptoms helped her parents to let pass their objections against the husband. The daughter could legally skip classes, and the patient's family conflict had become background noise only.

Symptomatic behaviour may be functional in an imbalanced relationship. We may expect such relationships to decompensate when the gain is removed before problems have been resolved. Resistance and crisis are to be expected when gain is removed before the patient has gained adaptive coping mechanisms to take its place. Secondary gain and reinforcement of symptoms may best be seen as a kind of social capital that allows for shifting secondary gain from symptom to desired behaviour. For example, attention and reinforcement may be replaced from voice hearing itself to coping with voices; voice hearing is no longer given full attention, instead the patient is stimulated to start coping exercises, while full attention is given after having fulfilled the exercises.

Step 10: Assess which coping strategies have been tried and their efficacy

Have coping strategies been applied consistently? Did the patient stop using them, and if so, for what reason? Assess the Coping Voices Inventory (CVI, Appendix 3; Jenner and Geelhoed-Jenner, 1998), a self-report inventory designed to determine the patient's habitual coping repertoire. The Maastricht Assessment of Coping Strategies (MACS; Bak *et al.*, 2001) may also be used. However, the MACS does not assess attributions, intent and agency: items that offer essential information for tailoring therapy. Compliance with coping strategies strongly depends upon the patient's attributions of power to the AVH. The effect of coping training is related to its consistent application. The degree to which someone struggles against the voices depends not only on his or her ability but also on what the patient wants. The patient's severity of symptoms and suffering, and his or her readiness for cooperation are probably more relevant than diagnosis.

Step 11: Estimate the levels of reluctance and disability

'Manipulative' behaviour should be respected as a desperate move made by an individual who sees no better option. Persons who are unable to escape feelings of shame or guilt, or who do not possess adaptive techniques for making their problems the subject of discussion or are unable to solve their problems may see manipulations as their only option. A person's suffering tends to elicit help from others. When you become sick, you stay in bed. Others are fairly likely to bring you food, allow you to stay at home, not to go to work/school, and not to participate in regular tasks. After a day or two, you will probably get up and go back to your business, either because you have actually got better or because you have been sick long enough to decide you became sick of staying ill.

But what if you decide not to get out of bed? In this case, your key figures will have to make a judgement. Are you refusing to get up because you are too sick to function normally? Or, have you just become lazy, stubborn, or . . . ? We distinguish between people who decline to do something due to disability and those who decline to do something because they are disinterested or unwilling. One does not ask a paralysed person to take out the trash, does one? But we do ask, or insist when it comes to someone who is refusing to take out the trash due to laziness.

How should we react when the reason behind some troublesome behaviour is indistinct or we are unsure whether we are faced with a case of disability or a case of unwillingness? The reason behind behaviour can be difficult to determine, especially in cases of illness or disorder. In these ambiguous cases, the therapist, the patient's friends, family and society at large have to decide whether or not the patient has a duty to do whatever he or she can to prevent disturbing behaviours, to recover or to cope with disabilities. The HIT model assumes that people do have such a duty up to their abilities.

Nevertheless, problems remain about degree and timing. People who are sick do deserve to be cut some slack; the question is for how much time and to what degree. A patient with the flu is entitled to some orange juice, toast and a fresh newspaper in bed. But we eventually ask him to get out of bed and come to the table. If he does not, we put pressure on him. The balance between gain (orange juice, toast in bed) and pressure (disapproval, gradual withdrawal of gains) influences the duration of illness.

When considering whether to give someone leeway on account of a disability or hold them to typical societal obligations, one should consider the specific nature of the disability. For what reason are we letting the patient off the hook in this particular instance? A patient with a sore knee may be exempt from carrying heavy loads, but it does not prevent him or her from peeling potatoes. Similarly, we may tolerate mistrust from a person who hears voices telling them we are out to get them, and yet expect that same person to be polite towards us. In all cases, remember that frequent changes in response are operantly conditioning the problem.

Assessment instruments for AVH-related psychiatric disorders

In functional psychoses, hallucinations are viewed as symptoms of psychiatric disorders. Patients do not always recognize their hallucinations as perceptional disturbances. The conviction of their realness may persist after disappearance of the hallucination. This is called delusional perception. Some authors consider hallucinations to be disturbances of interpretation rather than of perception (Frith, 1992; West, 1975). They postulate hallucinations as being mental images: an activity of thought that is being ineffectively and uncritically tested. Hence, impression and unconscious expectation are imperfectly filtered, or inaccurately interpreted. A variety of instruments are available for the classification of related psychiatric disorders and social functioning. This chapter will mention the ones that were used in HIT research: DES and DIS-Q for dissociative experiences; PANSS, WHO-SCAN (Schedule for Clinical Assessment in Neuropsychiatry) for psychiatric diagnoses; GSDS (Groningen Social Disabilities Scale) for social functioning; WHO-QoL brief for quality of life, and Illness Effects Questionnaire (IEQ) for burden on the family.

Dissociation Experiences Scale

The DES is a 28-item self-report scale to be used by persons of 18 and above. It consists of two parts. Part I is on sociodemographics, part II on dissociative experiences.

Dissociation Questionnaire

The DIS-Q is a 63-item self-report (rated on a 5-point scale) questionnaire consisting of two parts similar to the DES. It consists of four subscales: confusion of identity, loss of control, amnesia, and increased concentration/absorption.

Positive and Negative Symptom Scale

The PANSS consists of a 30-item, semi-structured patient interview on psychiatric symptoms existing the week prior to the interview. Items are rated by the investigator on a 7-point scale. We use five PANSS dimensions, derived from a large factor analytic study: positive and negative symptoms, disorganization, depression and excitement.

Schedule for Clinical Assessment in Neuropsychiatry (SCAN) and mini-SCAN

The SCAN is a semi-structured interview rooted in Anglo-Saxon tradition with focus on phenomenology. Its in-depth exploration with probing and exploring of symptoms in terms of severity, frequency, and interference is different from the 'yes' or 'no' approach of interviews such as Composite International Diagnostic Interview (CIDI; Haro *et al.*, 2006) and Structured Clinic Interview for DSM (SCID; Riskind *et al.*, 1987).

The mini-SCAN (Nienhuis, 2011), based on the SCAN, has kappa values around 0.90, except for the class of affective psychosis that has moderate inter-rater agreement. Advantage of the mini-SCAN is gain in time: 1 day training versus 4 days SCAN training and mean duration of interview: 25 minutes shorter than SCAN. Because of the clinical approach HIT prefers SCAN and mini-SCAN above other instruments.

WHO Quality of Life Scale brief

This is a 26-item self-report questionnaire. Two questions refer to quality of life and satisfaction with health, while the other 24 items are grouped into four domains: physical, psychological, social relationships and environment. The patient has to rate his or her satisfaction (with life, sleep, support, etc.) or experience (enjoying life, meaningfulness of life, safety, etc.) on a 5-point scale over the last two weeks. Total score is the sum of all 26 items (maximum 130).

Illness Effects Questionnaire

The IEQ measures relatives' subjective and objective consequences of being involved with someone with chronic psychiatric symptoms. The questionnaire has 45 items on: relational tension, attention, supervision, patient activation, and concern. Other questions regard financial consequences related to drugs, travelling, damaged goods, debts and so on. There are also questions regarding children, personal restrictions in personal life, etc.

Groningen Social Disabilities Scale

This is a semi-structured interview with the patient measuring social functioning and adjustment over the last four weeks, covering eight social roles: work and occupation, social relationships, involvement in society, household, relations with the family and the partner, parent role and self-care. Additional information from case managers or medical files is used too. Social disability is rated by the investigator on a 4-point scale from no, minimal, obvious to serious disability. Total disability scores are calculated by combining seven role scores excluding the parental role because of limited applicability.

Cases illustrating the HIT diagnostic procedure

Three cases can be used to illustrate the value of the HIT 11-step diagnostic system.

Case vignette: John

John was 6 years of age when his behaviour changed from one day to the next. When asked why, he answered that he heard commanding voices. For the past 2 years, John had begun stealing and displaying episodes of aggressiveness. For example, he stole candy from his brother Philip. On Sundays, he ate Philip's meat while his family was saying grace. His misbehaviour ran parallel with his voice hearing. It appeared that he started hearing these voices after the death of his grandfather. He had been diagnosed as conduct disorder suspect for child psychosis. Because neither cognitive behaviour therapy, play therapy nor medication had helped, he was referred to my voices clinic.

The first session was a family session. They were a traditional family: John, brother Philip (aged 12 years), mother (part-time nurse) and father (full-time carpenter). Both children did well at school and participated in extracurricular sports. No psychiatric disorder was found. John heard several voices: one commanding, none familiar to him. Asked whether he liked his AVHs or wanted to get rid of them, John reported to dislike them. A discrepancy between verbal (feeling guilty) and non-verbal (glowing eyes) communication was noticed, suggestive for ambivalence about his AVHs. Close scrutiny of John's AVHs and their consequences suggested possible secondary gain and selective reinforcement. The parents accepted John's misbehaviour because he was ill; hence not to be blamed. His voices commanded him to misbehave. Strikingly, John's voices only appeared when he did not get what he wanted. His parents let him have his way. Irrespective of their initial cause, John's AVHs seemed to have become an excuse for his misbehaviour and his attempts to get his own way at the expense of others. His parents' empathy might have reinforced his behaviour.

We implemented the following treatment. John was advised to resist his AVHs as much as he could, but not to worry when he failed. In case of failure in resisting eating his brother's cake, John had to apologize and buy Philip a new piece of cake using his own allowance. John's parents were asked to supervise this programme. Within a week, the commanding AVHs disappeared, while other voices remained. These disappeared with a coping programme and training the parents in selective reinforcement.

This case illustrates the diagnostic value of focused assessment, and its preventive potential (stigmatization with psychosis was prevented).

Case vignette: Miss Pedroni

Miss Pedroni (aged 14 years) was referred because of school absenteeism. At intake, the reason appeared to be her mother, who had been diagnosed with severe social phobia and sexual abuse-related PTSD. At her daughter's intake, the mother appeared to be having frightening visions of shades and abuse and had had threatening AVHs for years. The 11-step assessment revealed her to see flying kitchen utensils that spoke to her, and a delusional system suggesting schizophrenia. In reaction to her 'panic attacks' she called her husband who ordered the daughter to take care of her mother. The daughter called her grandparents to help. The result was that, except for the disturbing signs, all benefitted: the daughter could stay at home, which decreased mother's anxiety about being on her own. Also, the disturbed relations between husband and her parents were solved. In addition the daughter could legally fail to attend school.

In conclusion, focused assessment changed the diagnosis and therapy from the daughter to the mother's schizophrenia spectrum disorder and HIT.

Case vignette: Anton

Two years ago, Anton (aged 21 years) was diagnosed with schizophrenia. His condition improved with medication and intensive aftercare. However, behavioural problems resurfaced. He was referred to us after physical fighting with his stepfather and breaking furniture. Anton, his (step)parents and his regular therapist blamed his schizophrenia for the outbursts. Proper assessment revealed additional drug abuse-related AVHs, and his stepfather demanding his mother to stop paying for her son's drugs with a threat of leaving her. Detailed AVH assessment revealed a pattern similar to the above case studies: AVH appearance was related to conflicts, and disappeared when Anton got his way. Anton's stepfather refused to support Anton's soft drug habits and Anton started fighting, resulting in him getting money from his mother. Anton claimed a lawful right for drug money from his mother on the grounds that parents need to care for their children. He had never attempted to channel his aggressiveness. He rejected aggression-management therapy.

Given the choice between following such a programme or being reported for assault he chose the programme. This programme in combination with discussions about house rules, the introduction of stricter behavioural expectations and the involvement of his parents in the HIT programme reduced the AVHs and aggression.

Medication and compliance

HIT advises voice hearers to try medication on indication. Rejection is regretted, but accepted. Prescriptions are in accordance with the Dutch Psychiatric Association guidelines, which are fairly similar to the American Psychiatric Association's guidelines, and related to diagnosis (i.e. antipsychotics for patients with schizophrenia spectrum disorder and mood stabilizers for patients with affective disorder with antipsychotic addition when indicated). Patients are strongly advised to be careful with benzodiazepines, and to stop taking them after 10 consecutive days of use.

Medication compliance of schizophrenia patients is low. Non-compliance may rise from 48% in the first year to 74% thereafter (Corrigan et al., 1990). From 15 to 33% of admitted patients are non-compliant. Compliance may be improved by making home visits, frequent contacts and involvement of key figures. In my experience, linking past improvement with medication compliance may improve further compliance. Patients who accept the illness model are given psychoeducation about neurotransmitters, the role of cognitive deficits in perception and interpretation of stimuli. Traumatized voice hearers feel understood with an explanation of voices as post-traumatic reliving and remembrances.

Compliance has been found to be greater in internal than external attribution to the cause of the illness. Patients who believe in biological causes are more medication compliant than those who believe in psychosocial causes. This may be used in motivating patients for medication.

Non-compliance is persistent, and no effective strategy has been discovered yet. However, some rules of thumb may be tried:

- Optimize communication by: assessing reasons for non-compliance, neutralizing guilt feelings, relabelling non-compliance as a request for adjustment, a proper positive attitude, even when negativism is at stake, Socratic linking medication with improvement, and reinforcement with tokens.
- Educate to the point.
- Aim at acceptance.
- Start coping training.
- Stimulate internal attribution.
- Avoid deterrence and guilt feelings.
- Make use of companions.
- Apply instructive DVDs, apps, etc.
- Apply reminders.
- Reduce the number of drugs, the number of doses per day, and the number of pills per take.

In summary, the customer is always right; syrup catches more bees than vinegar; no patient objects against understanding; positive labels are better accepted than negative confrontations; avoid conflicts and do well; do not make irrevocable pronouncements; getting patients to agree with you is far more effective than being absolutely right; prevent contractual splits, but keep in touch; new rounds give new chances; and setting an example makes patients follow your lead.

Motivation strategies may improve medication compliance. Specific strategies are selected according to the patient's stage of readiness to change, their usual behaviour pattern and personality traits, and the presence and content of psychotic reasoning. Preferably, medication advice is not given before an extensive discussion about the problems associated with AVHs and the successes of HIT in other patients. If clinical conditions allow, prescription can best be postponed until the patient has entered the stage of action.

One important strategy is positive labelling. For example, non-compliance may be relabelled (in lieu of confrontation) as a form of cooperation, as a way of requesting advice for adjusting medication. In accordance with the patient's worldview and delusional system, medication may be offered as a protective shield against physical intrusions or alien intruders. First, increase the patient's burden by selective questioning. Second, ask for his or her wish to get rid of this. Third, talk to the patient about Faraday's cage, and elaborate on the cage's protective powers against waves. Fourth, regret that such a cage cannot be used without the user being labelled crazy. Fifth, elaborate on the blessings of having a chemical equivalent of Faraday's cage. Finally, give some examples of patients who have applied a chemical substitute successfully and wait for the patient's reaction. If the patient rejects the substitute nothing has been lost, but if he or she jumps at the substitute a winning situation has occurred.

Similarly, the effect of suggesting fortified wines to patients who feel overwhelmed by voices has been described earlier. Another example we gave was the taking of medication in order to protect a beloved person.

Coping training

The results of coping behaviour intervention studies are equivocal. This may be partly due to lack of a uniform coping classification system. Another complication in measuring the effectiveness of coping behaviour is that voice hearers apply similar coping behaviours with quite different, person-dependent intentions and attributions. The literature gives little information about constructing the ideal coping package. For example, what makes singing effective? Is it the vocal cords activity itself (Inouye and Shimizu, 1970), the spiritual content of hymns, the distraction, or is it just a matter of consistent implementation? What roles do former experiences, induction of alpha brain waves and belief play? On coping lists, voice hearers rank listening to music high as an applied coping strategy. However, many psychiatric patients listen to music all the time – as do many healthy citizens – without intending to use it to cope with voices.

Nevertheless, voice hearers and their relatives report positively about the HIT coping training. This involves teaching patients and relatives a repertoire of skills for anxiety management, distracting attention from the voices, and focusing attention on voices and evoking them when indicated. It is important to keep in mind that most voice hearers cope insufficiently and inconsistently (Geelhoed-Jenner *et al.*, 2001).

Because patients may apply the same coping behaviour with completely different intentions and attitudes and with completely different results (Geelhoed-Jenner *et al.*, 2001), HIT's coping training begins with an evaluation of the effectiveness of current coping strategies through daily monitoring (Jenner and Geelhoed-Jenner, 1998). The voice hearer's habitual coping pattern is assessed with the CVI (Appendix 3) and daily monitoring of the characteristics of the voices, their contextual aspects, the patient's coping behaviours and their effects.

Monitoring the habitual coping pattern has been found to be crucial for developing an appropriate set of coping strategies. Relatives are requested to monitor which signs of AVH they notice, the contextual aspects of the AVHs, their reactions towards the voice hearer, and their effects as well as the impact of the AVHs upon themselves. As a next step, the voice hearer draws up on the CVI which coping behaviours he or she has applied. The items cover the domains vocal (e.g. speaking, singing), motor (e.g. walking, cycling), cognitive (e.g. re-attribution, thought stop), physical (e.g. ear plug, automutilation), social (e.g. withdrawal, contacting, bargaining), physiological (e.g. sleeping, relaxation), spiritual (e.g. meditation, prayer) and chemical (e.g. alcohol, medication, eating). The items encompass diversion, withdrawal and actions as well as talking to and with voices. The frequency of application, whether this has been done consequently, and beneficial and/or ineffective effects are monitored for each item. The items endorsed by the patient are then categorized as anxiety reducing, distractive or focusing-on-voices, according the divisions made by Bentall *et al.* (1994). Be aware of the risk of abusing voices that are representations of self-hate, guilt or inferiority feelings. In these cases, the coping technique of abusing voices means self-abuse and may be ego-destructive.

The coping behaviour of many voice hearers, especially those with schizophrenia and borderline personality disorder, has been characterized as the inconsistent application of a wide variety of coping techniques with a preference for the least effective methods (Carter *et al.*, 1996; Cohen and Berk, 1985; Jenner, 2012a, 2012b; Sayer *et al.*, 2000). Lobban *et al.* (2004) found a significant association between illness awareness and course of the disease, but not between coping and course. Voice hearers cope more defensively when they experience their voices as negative. Voices experienced as positive are associated with a more active and cooperative coping style.

Based on the data from the habitual coping monitoring, appropriate coping strategies are selected, constructed into a coping strategy and then tested *in vivo*. It is best to start with simple behaviour such as vocal cord exercises (humming or singing). In my experience listening to music on a digital music device without vocal cord movement is ineffective. The effect of vocal cord exercises can be strengthened by selecting certain songs. This selection is highly personal. Some choose Christmas carols because of the association with happy days. Others go for battle songs, religious tunes or anthems connected with their sports club. Sometimes shy or timid patients may select songs with powerful messages, for example 'We are the champions'. These examples illustrate the extra value that selection may offer to the inner speech theory behind the use of vocal cords. Personal selection induces re-attribution, amplifies positive expectation and may prevent this coping becoming downgraded to no more than a kind of musical wallpaper. The chances of compliance may be increased by psychoeducation about the mechanisms of inner speech and counterstimulation.

As discussed earlier, an optimal coping strategy consists of a combination of anxiety management, distraction and focusing on the voices. The latter aims at active communication with the voice(s). This is quite different from both regular psychiatric practice and the neglect and avoidance most voice hearers regularly practice. Personification of the voices may aid in organizing focusing strategies, and in choosing the most appropriate ones. Attraction and feasibility are probably the best selection criteria.

Finally, the experimental stage is entered. A period of trial and error is begun with testing the effects of coping packages of about three coping behaviours for 4–6 consecutive weeks per package. A combination of vocal, cognitive and one other class of coping behaviour is advised. HIT applies a three-step coping package: Step 1 (usually vocal cord activities) takes 3 minutes. If successful, stop procedure, apply self-reinforcement. If not, continue with step 2. Step 2 – cognitive intervention – takes 5 minutes. If successful, stop procedure, apply self-reinforcement. If not, continue with step 3. Step 3 – motor activity – takes 15 minutes. If successful, stop procedure, apply self-reinforcement. If not, next time, new chances and self-reinforcement for perseverance.

Success parameters are individually, and exactly determined (tailor-made). For example: shorter duration, less loudly, lower intensity of burden (measured on a 10-points scale), less annoying, and so on. Key figures are advised to stimulate the voice hearer to cope whenever they notice him hearing voices. They change attention from voice hearing to coping, and reinforce the patient too. They are trained in *selective* reinforcement, and in giving support whenever setbacks occur.

Be aware of pitfalls

First pitfall, patients report that coping did not work. Reaction: ask patients for a detailed report of their coping trial. For some patients the report will demonstrate that they have not tried at all. My regular reply is something like: 'How can one tell a meal isn't tasty when one hasn't tasted?', followed by another round of motivation and emphasis on the association between effort and success. Other patients have stopped before coping step 3. They may need extra motivational interventions. More intensive and continuous stimulation and the support of relatives may also help. The third category is patients who are dissatisfied with the result. They get the discount reaction described above.

The second pitfall is using the wrong order of coping steps. Reaction: put the most attractive coping behaviour at step 1. This will motivate the voice hearer to start coping. One may consider that putting the most attractive coping at step 3 may act as a reward, but it is not most of the time. Imagine what happens if the least attractive step 1 is successful. Then, the patient is punished because (s)he is not given the chance to try the favourite coping behaviour. This situation most probably results in steps 1 and 2 being rushed through in order to get a chance of performing the desired step 3, or even worse the patient drop-outs.

Some coping monitor schemes may be illustrative. The imaginary patient in the example here is aiming at a two-point reduction in intensity. She may stop coping when her goal is achieved. Patients monitor four areas and the results are recorded in table form: (i) Voices say . . . (ii) Intensity of suffering before (I,1) and after (I,2) coping (on a scale of 1 to 10), (iii) Duration (in minutes) of the coping strategies applied (strategies 1–3), and (iv) whether Self-reinforcement has been applied.

Coping scheme 1 illustrates insufficient coping; neither steps 2 and 3 nor self-reinforcement have been applied.

Coping training monitoring scheme 1

Voices say:	$I(1)$	Duration of coping strategy 1	$I(2)$	Self-reinforcement
Slut!! Kill yourself	9	2 min	9	
		Duration of coping strategy 2	$I(2)$	
		Duration of coping strategy 3	$I(2)$	

Scheme 2 illustrates laziness in coping step 3, plus forgetting self-reward at all.

Coping training monitoring scheme 2

Voices say:	$I(1)$	Duration of coping strategy 1	$I(2)$	Self-reinforcement
Slut!! Kill yourself	9	2 min	8	
		Duration of coping strategy 2	$I(2)$	
	8	5 min	8	
		Duration of coping strategy 3	$I(2)$	
	8	3 min (raining)	8	

Schemes 3 and 4 illustrate the consequences of self-reinforcement. The patient in scheme 3 had reached 2 intensity degrees less so step 3 was not necessary. The goal for the patient in scheme 4 was to reduce intensity below 5. She was rewarded for completing all steps, but was stimulated to implement reinforcement. The 20% gain for scheme 5 requires the discount approach as well as a new round of motivation.

Coping training monitoring scheme 3

Voices say	I(1)	Duration of coping strategy 1	I(2)	Self-reinforcement
Slut!! Kill yourself	9	2 min	8	yes, . . .
		Duration of coping strategy 2	I(2)	
	8	5 min	7	yes, . . .
		Duration of coping strategy 3	I(2)	
		unnecessary		

Coping training monitoring scheme 4

Voices say	I(1)	Duration of coping strategy 1	I(2)	Self-reinforcement
Slut!! Kill yourself	9	2 min	8	yes, . . .
		Duration of coping strategy 2	I(2)	
	8	5 min	7	
		Duration of coping strategy 3	I(2)	
	7	15 min (raining)	7	

Coping training monitoring scheme 5

Voices say	I(1)	Duration of coping strategy 1	I(2)	Self-reinforcement
Slut!! Kill yourself	10	2 min	8	
		Duration of coping strategy 2	I(2)	
	8	5 min	8	
		Duration of coping strategy 3	I(2) no, doesn't work	
		Stopped the coping training at second trial		

As mentioned earlier, it is safe to start with simple and congruent items such as singing, distraction and physical activities. Evoking voices, a hypercongruent focusing action, may be advised when congruent strategies give insufficient relief. Severe psychotic states may be indications for hypercongruent focusing actions. Evoking may induce strong emotions and anxiety, not least in relatives. Hence, the first focusing session should always be conducted in the therapist's presence, preferably in the presence of relatives too. Later on, patients may practise focusing exercises at their homes. I prefer to deal at length with the steps the patient considers taking when undesirable aliens are invading his house as an introduction. Next, alternative measures are extensively discussed. This round is concluded with: 'OK, you could ask the intruders why they do so, could ask them to leave, could hide yourself or could call the police, and so on. Isn't it strange that you don't do any of these when voices enter your head? Wouldn't it be time to take action and show your voices who is in command, to regain being boss in your brain?' Most of my patients agree, and become willing to start taking action.

There are many focusing techniques that can be used. These vary from asking the voices questions, thanking them for giving advice, negotiations, through confrontation with mistakes, blaming them for unreliability to bullying or scolding them till evocation. In evocation, the voice hearer is advised to evoke his voices at moments that he feels (fairly) well. The consequences of evocation are predictable: the voices may either appear, stay away or blame the therapist as unreliable. Therapeutic interpretations are as predictable. Occurrence of voices may be interpreted as the first possible sign of the voice hearer's power and his return to command. The patient's doubt and disbelief are relabelled as forms of modesty, and challenging the voices again is strongly recommended. The next step is to ask the voices about their 'identity' and credibility. They are also asked about their intentions. Positive voices may be asked for information about the negative ones, even for help against these. The voices staying away or not answering may be interpreted as their fear of losing control. Repeating the evocation is recommended here too. Each trial increases the patient's belief in his growing power and enhances his self-reliance. Voices that blame the therapist may be countered with examples of their unreliability. For this reason, evoking voices preferably follows the in-depth analysis of voice characteristics.

In the end, the patient's preferences and monitoring data help in effectively tailoring the coping package. Time, perception and effect monitoring serves two goals: the fine-tuning of the coping strategy and providing information about whether and how the strategy was implemented.

A final coping strategy is based on the principle of keeping elements that work and replacing those that do not work. Following psychoeducation about learning theory, relatives are trained in selectively reinforcing the voice hearers' attempts at implementing their coping behaviours. Monitoring by relatives provides the therapist with data for support, coaching and selective reinforcement. *In vivo* trials of coping behaviour take time. Therefore, the inter-session interval is increased from 2–4 weeks to 4–6 weeks during the coping training period.

Cognitive behavioural interventions in HIT

Cognitive behavioural therapy, which is discussed further in Chapter 6, is based on learning theories. HIT selectively applies some CBT interventions and operant conditioning. Learning theory postulates that expectations, assumptions and mis-interpretations of voice hearers are important in the continuation of AVHs. CBT applies the ABC postulate as described in Chapter 6.

Most voice hearers presume that their negative expectations are becoming realized; they strikingly test this presumption in an insufficient and inconsistent manner, or may even lack any testing. The aim of cognitive behavioural interventions is, among other things, changing the voice hearer's interpretation of voices as powerful and malevolent (Chadwick and Birchwood, 1994). The focuses of CBT are (a) changing the attribution from external causes into internally generated ones, and labelling them as just annoying symptoms, (b) contesting the power of the voices by examining their predictive power and disobedience to command hallucinations, and (c) removing the supposed meaning of voices and reducing them to annoying noise. Interventions that work may increase mastery and control, as well as reduce secondary negative emotions.

Cognitive behavioural interventions in HIT focus on making sense of the AVHs, on precipitating events, on emotional, cognitive and behavioural actions, and on the reactions of relevant others. In contrast with most CBT programmes, relatives are actively involved in the process. Other differences are the flexibility of HIT versus the rather strict CBT protocols and the pragmatic HIT explanation of voices versus the psychiatrically coloured one applied in CBT. When voice hearing is related to past traumatic events, AVH may cause the recall of negative memories that may be selectively increased through operant conditioning. If this is the case, counter-conditioning may be indicated. Also, eye movement desensitization and reprocessing (EMDR) may be applied. For patients whose voices have become a link in a sequence of fear and avoidance, *in vivo* behaviour experiments that challenge incorrect assumptions may be indicated. Interventions that work may increase mastery and control, as well reduce secondary negative emotions. Whatever the intervention, Socratic reasoning remains the preferred style of communication. It is an effective approach for inserting doubt about beliefs and mis-interpretations, and is effective in patients who are uncertain of being in the right in my experience. In contrast, 100% deluded convictions remain resistant to CBT.

In HIT, voice hearers are encouraged to monitor the voices and triggering events, the intensity of experienced interference, and the reactions of others. Also caregivers receive cognitive interventions. They monitor their interactions with the voice hearer and are given training in applying successfully selective reinforcement (for monitoring, see Appendix 4).

Operant conditioning

Successes reinforce behaviour, motivate further effort and indirectly help with compliance. Hence, in HIT tasks are split into as many small steps as possible. This is done because the smaller the task, the less the chance of failure; more small steps allow for more possibilities of reinforcement than one big one; and whereas the success from a big task takes a long time to come round, instant success can be expected from small steps. In addition, selective operant conditioning may improve low self-esteem and strengthen defective ego functions.

Operant conditioning can also be applied to minimize drop-out. Voice hearers who comply and do homework tasks are seen frequently.

As described earlier, the HIT inter-session interval may be extended in voice hearers. This may be done in patients who show passive resistance, those who fail to do homework tasks, those who seem to become fearful and those who do not take the necessary steps. Unintentionally, these patients may be harmed by continuation of the regular frequency. Although they need sufficient time to weigh up the pros and cons, they also need sufficient information to decide whether or not to take the step. In such cases continuation of sessions may maintain the problem instead of helping it to be solved. Discussion of their burden has become symptomatic; discussing has become the substitute of trying.

HIT's systems approach

As mentioned earlier, family treatment has been deliberately selected in HIT. The therapy integrates elements of the problem solving, psychoeducation, social constructivism, strategic and narrative family treatment schools. I have noticed that each patient system requires its own optimal mixture. Joint patient–relatives sessions are favoured, although separate individual sessions may be held when indicated. Also, additional sessions with important others (e.g. other therapists, the police, and case managers) are organized when indicated.

Following Michael White's narrative approach, voices are personified with questions to both patient and relatives (White, 1986). What have the voices done to you? What has been and is their impact on your social life, your work, and so on? Voices are made part of the system: they are relabelled allies, enemies or negligible.

Relatives are trained in positive labelling, and selectively reinforcing the patient's coping efforts, self-care and daily activities. Monitoring helps them to gain insight into the effects of their own behaviour, which makes them more open to adjustments that may lower the level of expressed emotion. Lower expressed emotion is known to lead to a better prognosis.

HIT's psychoeducation

The primary target of HIT psychoeducation is the voice hearing itself. Information about psychiatric disorders is adjusted depending upon the patient's insight into and acceptation of mental illness and their attitude and readiness towards psychiatric diagnoses and treatment. HIT psychoeducation includes: epidemiological facts about voice hearing, summaries of relevant theories such as subvocalization, neurotransmitters, treatment efficacy, links between trauma and AVHs, and the impact of AVHs on voice hearer and relatives. The timing and order of these lectures depend upon the stages of illness awareness, coping behaviour and treatment process.

In HIT the psychoeducation is tailored to the voice hearer and his or her system. Lecturing on general information is rarely done, and group classes are incidental. In contrast, HIT psychoeducation is given in bite-sized chunks that relate to the topic relevant to the stage of therapy reached. In the diagnostic stage, explanations are given about inner speech, fMRI findings, brain procedures for selecting between in and outside the body, and so on. We always assess trauma. Simultaneously, psychoeducation on present knowledge of this subject is given and a trauma questionnaire (TRAMAL: Appendix 5) is offered. HIT psychoeducation is related to symptoms and signs, while diagnosis-related psychoeducation is given on indication only. Selective reinforcement and operant conditioning are explained during the introduction to coping training.

What goals does HIT aim for with psychoeducation?

Psychoeducation is a best-practice pillar of mental health. Refraining from psychoeducation is seen as a great mistake. Several researchers have demonstrated that psychoeducation improves knowledge of disorders. Beyond that, results have been equivocal. There are at least three assumptions behind psychoeducation: (1) Information reduces stressful rumination. (2) Psychoeducation enhances insight, which improves treatment compliance. (3) Insight predicts a better prognosis. However, each pre-supposition may be questioned.

Better knowledge of severe psychiatric disorders may be shocking and frightening for patients and relatives. Psychoeducation in these cases can lead to denial and avoidance of help, two factors that are common in patients with schizophrenia spectrum disorders. Here, psychoeducation may be counterproductive.

Psychoeducation of friends and family may lead to their greater participation in the patient's treatment. However, the more intensive the contact between patient and key figures, the smaller the positive effect (Holmes et al., 1999). Effect size partly depends on the person's prior familiarity with the very content psychoeducation is designed to familiarize them with. Gender is also relevant. Psychoeducation about violent tendencies of psychiatric patients appeared to influence perceptions of violent male patients, but not of violent females (Penn et al., 1999). Psychoeducation influences a subject's perception of patients in general, but not the perception of any single patient (Penn et al., 1999). Giving subjects information about violent behaviour of patients with schizophrenia, other psychiatric disorders and the general population has greater destigmatizing effects than educating subjects on violent behaviour of patients with schizophrenia only (Penn et al., 1999). Providing subjects with a general frame of reference for the condition of schizophrenia may not, by itself, be adequate to affect their impressions of newly encountered individuals with a psychiatric disorder.

An age-independent positive association has been found between insight, cooperation and compliance for several disorders. However, no relationship could be found between insight, severity of symptoms and compliance in patients with schizophrenia (Amador, 1994). Insight was related to social functioning, while symptoms but not insight improved with medication. The greater the patient's suffering, the earlier the therapeutic effect is perceived, and the greater its effect, the greater the patient's compliance. Another, compliance-enhancing factor is the strength of the therapeutic relationship. In general, treatment compliance in patients with chronic diseases and maintenance medication is relatively low.

While psychoeducation improves disease-related knowledge in patients and key figures, it has little positive effect on their behaviour. Trauer and Sacks (2000) found patient insight to be positively correlated with depression and negatively correlated with personal functioning. Amador *et al.* (1996) found temporary increased suicidal ideation after psychoeducation. Insight plus passive coping induces more depression than insight plus active coping in schizophrenic patients. In other words, psychoeducation may have (temporary) counterproductive effects. A programme on drug risks in the Netherlands demonstrated a possible paradoxical effect of psychoeducation. It resulted in a substantial increase in knowledge, but also increased curiosity and the number of students experimenting with drugs.

Family-oriented psychoeducation, on the other hand, led to increased knowledge, less rehospitalization, reduction of psychotic symptoms and improved social functioning in an RCT among Chinese patients with schizophrenia. The significantly better effects were mediated by reductions in level of expressed emotions (EE). Reduced EE may reduce the relapse rate in schizophrenia over time (Zheng Li and Arthur, 2005).

Stigmatization is a side-effect of the diagnosis psychosis. Stigma negatively correlates with quality of life and positive self-image, with a magnified effect in women. Therefore, psychoeducation about a diagnosis may require adjustment over time. Start with psychoeducation in general terms about diagnoses, next talk about training patients in coping. Finally discuss the diagnosis and the need for medication.

The main question in psychoeducation concerns how to adjust its form, timing and organization to decrease unwanted side-effects.

HIT psychoeducation: why and how?

Psychoeducation is intended to provide optimal information. However, expert knowledge of the causes, course, consequences and prognoses of disorders has changed tremendously in recent decades. Therapists are still divided among themselves about the most effective treatment programmes. For example, there is more emphasis on medication in the USA than in European countries. In Europe, a higher value is placed on problem-solving psychotherapies. In addition, patients and therapists differ in their views on which problems are the most important targets. The top 10 most important issues for patients are nearly the reverse of the top 10 list for therapists. Issues that friends and family find important fall in the middle. The degree of consent that can be achieved between parties determines the progress of therapy (Garfield, 1994). To achieve the desired effect, psychoeducation should be focused initially on creating consent. Motivational interviewing is more effective than confrontation and straightforward educational programmes. Another question concerns whether psychoeducation should be given in groups, individually or in families. Some friction is to be expected in the group setting due to the diversity of interests and stages of disease of individual attendees.

Optimal timing in HIT psychoeducation

Is it best to use a standard programme following a strict protocol, or should we attend and adjust to the patient's condition and wishes? Psychoeducation requires disorder specificity. The illness-awareness model (Prochaska and DiClemente, 1982) starts with selectively emphasizing suffering and symptoms. Next come casual remarks about the positive effects of medication, lifestyle adjustment, coping training and whatever else is relevant. This model places psychoeducation somewhat later in the therapeutic process than do most regular psychoeducation programmes.

Advertisement psychology has examined the effectiveness of forms of information transfer. Computerized and expert instructions have good effects. Goal-oriented information, skills training and reinforcement with direct feedback and reminders appear to be effective in changing behaviour patterns. Combining feedback with skills training and application training of specific protocols unmistakably changed the behaviour of family doctors. Combining distinct interventions improves results, especially in the patient. Clearer and more detailed instructions, video and frequent role-playing predict greater effects. The efficacy of leaflets and formal lectures is almost negligible, as are the effects of discussing case files, and patient feedback with specialists. Unclear tasks and goals frustrate both trainer and trainees. If we are to take these findings seriously, we have to make great changes in the standard psychoeducation model. HIT tries to do so by adjusting form, content and timing to the individual patient and his or her system.

We must differentiate between the educational needs of trainers and the learning needs of trainees. The success of training correlates with the conformity of both these needs. To that end, it would be worth examining the effectiveness of a psychoeducation programme designed by groups of patients, therapists and key figures.

The dialectic learning model distinguishes four types of learning: abstract, concrete, active and passive. Mixing these types in both teaching and material probably gives optimal results. Serial teaching is excellent for modelling logical steps in a linear sequence. Its disadvantage is that students rarely make connections between the material, anticipate results or recognize broader outlines. The holistic learning style better suits the last three skills.

Learning effects are rather short-lived. Enhancing duration of effects requires empathetic involvement, continuous support, crisis management, orientation towards problem solving, communication skills, and strengthening of the social network. Improvements in coping skills may be the best predictor of positive effect.

Studies show that psychoeducation programmes are numerous and widely variable. The family-oriented version appears to be the most effective. Multi-family versions perform best in relapse prevention and occupational rehabilitation. Some studies have found a 20–50% reduction in relapse and rehospitalization rates in patients with schizophrenia with intensity and duration of psychoeducation as crucial factors.

Rehabilitation

Social isolation, self-neglect and a lack of daily activities are common in voice hearers with a psychiatric disorder. HIT applies state-of-the-art rehabilitative interventions. However, it does not present these as 'rehabilitation' but as coping strategies (destigmatization), or as techniques that demonstrate the patient's decision to regain control of his or her brain (empowerment). This wording is carefully chosen in order to reduce resistance, stigma and non-compliance.

Case vignette

This patient was referred to me because of treatment-resistant voices. The start of treatment was far from easy: his psychiatrist had told him that continuation of his treatment was dependent on visiting the Voices Outpatient Department. One can imagine the patient's willingness and cooperation.

His unpleasant smell suggested severe hygienic problems. His story was full of paranoia: his neighbours were after him, his voices were organized by a consortium that cooperated with the police who conspired against him. He rejected any treatment. At least he consented to the idea of changing the agenda: bullying his voices instead of them pestering him. He enjoyed a plan to confuse the voices with an unexpected act. I suggested the following plan: 'You buy strong and pretty-smelling soap, take a shower and evoke your voices'. He was instructed to tell his voices firmly: 'I am taking over control now. You better take a look at what's happening to the lather. The same thing will happen to you if you don't stop bothering me'.

I hoped that the smell of soap could reduce both his foul smell and his neighbours' disapproval.

The next session, he enthusiastically reported his experience with this new technique. He had noticed a behaviour change in his neighbours that he related to his increasing control over his voices. As I had hoped, his general social functioning had improved (a little) as result of his new and more appealing smell. His voices reduced to once a week in the next three coping months, while conflicts with his neighbours occurred less. The police were no longer called in.

Multi-family HIT aftercare

Despite widespread HIT-induced improvements, deficits in social functioning may continue in chronic patients. Their negative symptoms do not sufficiently improve, and their control of voices tends to deteriorate over time. Multi-family HIT, a combination of HIT and McFarlane's multi-family treatment, has been developed as an aftercare training programme for these patients (Jenner *et al.*, 2006a). Training groups consist of 5–7 voice hearers, each accompanied by at least one relative or key figure. The programme starts with a 2-hour acquaintance and introduction session for all. Group rules are introduced, and a course book containing psychoeducation materials, homework tasks and diary cards is distributed. This session covers: welcome; introduction and points of departure; agreements, group rules and regulations; who is who; organization and form of training(days): skills training; use of monitoring forms and homework tasks. Then follows an intensive day programme once a week for some months, followed by a biweekly 4-hour training, that may be followed by monthly 2-hour sessions for as long as participants feel it is needed.

The training focuses on dealing with voices and the voice hearer, and planning daily actions. The training is divided into three parts, the first two mandatory, the third part optional. Trainers select the topics of the first part, group members select topics in the second and third parts. Trainers select homework tasks related to the topic of the day. Trainees monitor problems for which they seek the help of the other group members. At all sessions, each trainee reports for 5 minutes the problem he or she wants to bring forward. Then trainees select the topic of the day. Preference is given to crisis and urgent situations.

Educational forms are: lectures, group discussion, brainstorming, skills training and relaxation exercises. Educational tools are: trainer and trainee manuals, sheets, and PowerPoint presentations (Jenner *et al.*, 2001). The manuals describe each day's protocol.

Trainers follow their protocol manual of the day's programme in topics and time per item. The patient manual starts with explanations on: why this training, why homework has to be done, and the group rules. Next chapter is on psychosis and stress vulnerability, psychoeducation, relevant exercises and homework. Each chapter has blank pages for making notes. Chapters are on making a personal prevention plan, (dealing with) aggression, social support and social functioning, what should you tell others and when, handicap and/or obstruction-based behaviour; then changing your behaviour, drugs, constructing and keeping a day programme, problem solving, giving and receiving compliments. The training focuses on practice; issues come from inter-session problem monitoring.

Indications and contraindications for HIT

Indications of HIT are AVHs irrespective of their origin, duration and diagnosis. Contraindications are disorganization (of thought), word salad, inadequate mastery of language, and primary addictions.

Relative contraindications are subnormal intelligence and organic brain disorders. This contraindication is relative because there is clear evidence that HIT for people with learning difficulties is feasible and effective with some adjustments. For example there may need to be more focus on operant conditioning, mediation, coordination with relatives, flashcards and client-appropriate methods of communication.

Evidence for the effectiveness of HIT

The cost-effectiveness of HIT has been scientifically demonstrated (Jenner *et al.*, 1998, 2004, 2006b; Jenner and van de Willige, 2001; Stant *et al.*, 2003; Wiersma *et al.*, 2001, 2004), with a tendency towards an even better cost-ratio when implemented on a nationwide scale (Stant *et al.*, 2003). A naturalistic 4-year adults follow-up study ($N = 40$), a pilot adolescent study ($N = 14$), and an 18-month follow-up RCT ($N = 76$) have been conducted on the feasibility and effectiveness of HIT. A multi-family HIT aftercare programme has also been examined in a naturalistic study.

The first naturalistic study assessed 40 patients aged 20–62 years (mean age 37, SD 11 years) with a mean AVH duration of 8 years before visiting the Voice-hearers Outpatient Department at the University Medical Centre Groningen. One-third of the subjects had experienced AVHs for more than 10 years. Almost all had multiple symptoms, and 46% hallucinations in other sensory modalities too. The majority had been receiving mental health care for more than 5 years (20% more than 10). Past treatment refusal and non-compliance were common. Twenty-five per cent had a history of attempted suicide. Twenty-five subjects had a DSM-IV-TR diagnosis of schizophrenia, the others dissociative disorder or borderline personality disorder.

At the end of treatment, the patients reported significantly lower AVH frequencies and durations of negative content ($p < .001$). In total, 40% of them became completely free of AVHs. Over 50% had regained mastery of both AVHs and thoughts, while two-thirds reported that AVHs no longer interfered with their daily activities or caused them anxiety. The percentage of patients suffering from considerable anxiety, loss of control and interference with thinking and daily activities as measured by the AHRS decreased from 82% to 20%. In total, about 50–60% reported improvements in AVH-related consequences. Seventy-eight per cent were satisfied with their treatment, and 72% of treatments were ended by mutual consent (Jenner *et al.*, 1998).

Thirty-nine patients cooperated in a 4-year follow-up. At follow-up, over 70% rated their present health condition as fair to excellent. Eighteen per cent had remained free of voices. The number, frequency and duration of voices had dropped considerably over the follow-up period, but negative content appeared persistent in some cases. Suffering from voices as measured with the AHRS rose from 20% after treatment to 30% at follow-up. Compared to the end-of-treatment status, 50% of patients assessed their present state as better, 40% reported no change, and only 8% reported deterioration. All patients reported less suffering than before treatment. Although most patients still scored 4 or higher on the PANSS, antipsychotic medication could be decreased ($Z = -2.82, p = .005$). Social functioning as measured with the GSDS (Wiersma *et al.*, 1990) improved substantially in 41% of participants for daily activities and in about 20% for social contacts and relationships. Overall, sustained improvement was found in 67% of patients and another 26% experienced further improvement during the follow-up period (Wiersma *et al.*, 2004).

The results of the pilot study of 14 adolescents with early psychosis were equal to or better than in the above study. Compliance and satisfaction with HIT were good to high. After HIT, 65% became free of voices, and the majority demonstrated substantial improvement in mastery, anxiety, interference with thinking and social functioning (daily activities $N = 11$, work and study $N = 8$). No patient had worsened (Jenner and van de Willige, 2001).

Finally, a RCT comparing HIT with treatment as usual (TAU) was conducted with assessments at baseline (pretreatment), after 9 months of treatment (post-treatment) and at 18-month follow-up. The standard blind randomization was carried out by an independent medical technology unit of the university hospital. A statistical minimization procedure taking into account gender, chronicity of illness (more or less than 5 years) and severity of symptoms (with or without a PANSS-P rating of 5) was applied separately for two geographical areas (treatment centres). Seventy-six patients (37 in the HIT group) were included with DSM-IV diagnoses of paranoid schizophrenia (78%), schizoaffective disorder (15%) and psychosis not otherwise specified (NOS) (7%). Patients were assessed by research staff blind for treatment with the AHRS, PANSS, WHO-QoL brief and the GSDS. Sixty-three patients (83%) completed all three assessment waves. All intent-to-treat analyses were based on these patients. Nine per cent of patients were lost at the 9-month follow-up, rising to 16% at the 18-month follow-up. Drop-out rates did not differ significantly on any of the relevant baseline variables. No significant differences in medication dosage could be found pre- and post-treatment (Jenner *et al.*, 2004, 2006b).

HIT patients experienced significantly greater improvements in subjective burden of voices than TAU patients. Improvements in distress and total burden of the voices persisted at 18-month follow-up ($p < .05$). Improvements in negative content, distress and total burden persisted at 18-month follow-up. Post-treatment, HIT patients also improved significantly more than TAU patients on the PANSS subscales: positive symptoms ($p < .001$), disorganization ($p < .05$), general psychopathology ($p < .01$) and total PANSS score ($p < .01$). Effect sizes varied on these dimensions from 0.47 (depression) to 0.71 (hallucinations), and NNT from 2 (hallucinations) to 3–5 (depression, disorganization, and total score).

Post-treatment, HIT patients rated their quality of life as significantly better than TAU patients. At 18-month follow-up, 71% of HIT patients rated their quality of life (QoL) as 'good/very good' versus 58% of TAU patients. On the total QoL score, HIT patients improved steadily on almost every domain, while TAU patients did not. QoL was rated 5.4 points higher in the HIT group by the 18-month follow-up, while the TAU group ratings hardly changed (t = 2.11; p < .05; Wiersma et al., 2004).

Post-treatment, HIT patients had significantly improved in most areas of social functioning, against hardly any improvement in TAU patients. Improvements persisted at the 18-month follow-up assessment (NNT = 7). Evidently, disability was significantly reduced in five social functioning key areas. The percentage of HIT patients showing improved social functioning was generally twice as large as that of TAU patients, deterioration was twice as small (except for self-care). Half of the HIT patients improved more than 20% on their total social functioning score, against 15% of controls (p < .001). Clinically significant improvement in this chronic population was defined as post-treatment disability scores 3 or less. (A rating of 3 implies a serious disability with gross deviation from expected behaviour and a need for professional help.) At baseline, 76% of the HIT patients and 74% of the controls had at least one rating of 3 or above. Post-treatment, these proportions were reduced to 51% and 67% respectively. The number of HIT patients that improved was three times that of the controls (25% versus 7%). This trend persisted at 18-month follow-up. The HIT group had further improved during the follow-up period (though less so than during treatment) on all areas, except for relationship with partners. In the total study period, HIT patients improved significantly more than controls in functioning in household and family relationships (p < .05), and to a lesser degree in relationships with partners and parents and in occupational and daily activities. In the end, overall functioning in the HIT group improved 2.84 points, compared with 0.97 points in the TAU group (t = 2.09; p < .05).

Pre- and post-treatment, differences in mean dosage of antipsychotics, antidepressants and benzodiazepines were not statistically significant. However, at 18-month follow-up, mean dosage of antipsychotics was significantly higher (df = 56; t = −2.70; p = .009) in the TAU group (Wiersma et al., 2004).

In the pilot HIT multi-family treatment study (Jenner et al., 2006a), voice hearers improved distinctly in subjective burden, frequency of voice hearing, interference with daily activities and thinking (p < .05), and control over AVHs (p < .01). Improvements in PANSS scores occurred in the depression and excitement subscales (p = .05). Improvements were most pronounced for PANSS total score, positive symptoms and disorganization (p < .01). Social functioning improved in the domains: household tasks (p < .01), and in social contacts and integration in the community at 5% level. The total social functioning score showed improvements by about 20% (p < .01).

Improvements were also measured in all IEQ scores of relatives, reaching statistical significance in the domains dealing with patients' symptoms, adjustment to symptoms and general relationship with the patient.

Stepped-treatment approach

Further HIT rules of thumb:

- As short as is safe and possible, as comprehensive, complex and as long as is needed.
- Normalize, advise and control.

Case vignette

A 15-year-old girl was referred because of treatment-resistant AVHs. She has an autism spectrum disorder, an anxiety disorder and anxiety-provoking hallucinations. These symptoms disturb family and school life. She sleeps with her parents and fails to attend school. Her intelligence is sufficient for yearly moving up to the next form, but she is moody with aggressive outbursts. She is afraid of being alone at home.

We made use of monitoring and psychoeducation, challenging her autistic cocksureness, and changing the parents' selective reinforcement. Within four sessions she became free of hallucination as well as anxiety for dark places. She can now stay alone at home. Of course, she is still autistic.

In conclusion, she no longer has disturbing hallucinations, family life is improved and there is less family burden.

More serious and complex cases have been described throughout the book.

Part 3

HIT in specific target groups

Chapter 5

HIT and suicidal patients

The prevalence of hallucinations is high in patients with schizophrenia, depressive psychosis, and dissociative and borderline personality disorder. Suicide risk is high in all these disorders. Hence, a high association between AVHs and suicide is likely. In adolescents suicidal ideation and behaviour are 8 times higher in patients with AVHs than in those with identical diagnoses without AVHs, suggesting that AVH itself increases the suicidal risk (Kelleher *et al.*, 2012, 2013, 2014). The Kelleher group found that AVH predicts an ultra-high risk for suicide attempts. In adolescents, 34% had had at least one suicide attempt by the 1-year follow-up compared with 4% of the total adolescent population and 13% of adolescents with psychopathology without AVHs. Voice-hearing adolescents accounted for 80% of the acute suicide attempts. Suicidal attempts were threefold higher in adolescent psychiatric outpatients who reported psychotic symptoms compared with patients who did not; an eightfold higher risk was noted in patients diagnosed with major depressive disorder. The suicidal risk is more than momentary – the risk remains over time. Nearly one-half of children who reported psychotic symptoms at age 11 had attempted or completed suicide by age 38 (Fisher *et al.*, 2013).

HIT stages used

In HIT, regular procedures are applied to suicidal voice hearers. A pivotal role is given to crisis intervention with non-denouncing, non-rejecting and joining-in behaviour as the preferred style. In summary, the programme consists of: (i) empathetic listening, joining in and clear assessment of suicidal ideation and behaviour, (ii) relabelling suicidal ideation and behaviour, (iii) negotiations and dealing, (iv) multiple-choice programmes with (v) small steps. The approach consists of a nine-step programme, most of the stages of which are regarded as regular interventions and some of which are more HIT specific, such as: (a) semantic conditioning, (b) at the imaginary grave, (c) arranging the imaginary heritage, and (d) hypercongruent intervening (Jenner, 2013).

Stage 1: Making and keeping a therapeutic relationship

Any diagnosis or treatment will start with the formation of a therapeutic relationship.

Stage 2: Assessment

This includes assessment of motives, free will, dangerousness, death risk, crisis-generating and crisis-protecting factors. Suicidal risk assessment looks at: suicidal ideation; preparations and availability of means; concreteness of plans, such as place, time, farewell letter; psychiatric history; suicidal history; family history; lethality of (planned) method; addiction; changes in social behaviour; recent loss; life events, depression, hopelessness; and goals such as ending misery, taking revenge or a real death wish.

Although the reliability of risk scales is limited, suicide intent and risk–rescue scales may be used, provided the therapist knows their limitations. Other helpful scales are the Sad Person Scale and the No Hope Scale:

Sad Person Scale	No Hope Scale
Sex	No framework for meaning
Age	Overt change in clinical condition
Depression	Hostile interpersonal environment
Previous attempt	Out of hospital recently
Ethanol abuse	Predisposing personality factors
Rational thinking loss	Excuses for dying present and believed
Social support lacking	
Organized plan	
No spouse	
Sickness	

Stage 3: Statement about the law and your views

Give an explicit statement about the law and your personal ideas regarding a person's right(?) to commit suicide.

Stage 4: Semantic conditioning

This is an unusual but effective method of joining in. At the start, use words selectively that fit the emotional state of the suicidal person. Start with words (indirectly) related to death such as: deadly serious, dead endings, bleed to death, a stillborn plan, deathblow, dead tired, they have mentally sentenced you to death, scared to death, they have put you on a dead end, etc. Gradually you turn to words that refer to life at first with a negative component such as feeling lifeless, tired of life, lively report of misery that is told in a life-like way. Next, you change to more optimistic contents and feelings such as vitally important, life pattern, life span, and so on. Deliberately, words of misery are changed via lifeless towards livelihood. As is known from advertisement psychology, feelings may follow this change.

Stage 5: Discuss possible alternatives

Possible alternatives for reaching the suicidal person's goal are discussed, preferably congruently, but sometimes hypercongruency is indicated.

Some examples are given below for illustration.

At the imaginary grave

This intervention may be applied to suicidal voice-hearing patients who intend to take revenge by suicide (attempt) for being maligned. Maligning may lead to suicidal ideation. Some suicidal persons suffer from feeling maligned. They have a mistaken conviction of the impact of their suicidal behaviour. Continuous frantic but unsuccessful attempts to stop the maligners may induce the idea that a suicide may make these holy terrors, nuisances and bullies change their ways.

The imaginary grave procedure is as follows (Jenner, 2013):

- Step 1: Stimulate and evoke detailed expressions of degrading, hurting, offending and injuring situations.
- Step 2: Assess the person's reactions and coping behaviour, and the perpetrators' reactions. In cases of evil behaviour do not hesitate to aggravate the evil, and emphasize the unwillingness of the perpetrators to change and stop their hurting behaviour.
- Step 3: Show commitment and empathy. Then introduce the imaginary funeral and say to the patient: 'Imagine me standing at your grave. What do you think . . . (names of perpetrators) will do and say? Do they weep and repent or is there any chance they will say "He always was a coward and now he did not dare to live on?" Or do they feel relieved that you are gone and think or even say that your suicide made things tidy and neat again? What reaction do you consider most likely?'
- Step 4: Mirror the patient and discuss the chance that his suicide will probably overshoot the mark, with no chance to correct it: dead people can no longer adjust their plans.
- Step 5: Finally, discuss alternative actions that have greater chances of reaching the goal.

Case vignette: Arranging the imaginary heritage

Martha was referred because of suicidal behaviour. It appeared that she heard the voice of her cousin who had sexually abused her for more than 8 years since she was 8 years of age. At first, her parents did not believe her and she was referred to a child psychologist for pathological lying. Two years ago, her cousin was caught raping her. Instead of understanding, her family pressured her not to report her cousin to the police. Her cousin black-mailed her, stating she was a lesbian, which probably would have resulted in her being evicted by her orthodox Presbyterian parents and community. She was convinced that suicide was her only way out. She reacted neither to empathy nor to suggestions of change.

The communication went as follows.

Therapist: If the situation could be changed for the better would you continue to want to commit suicide?
Patient: There is no chance that my family will change.
Therapist: If you were in charge would you commit suicide?
Patient: Of course not.
Therapist: Then we follow the same track. Tell me what will the family do with your belongings?
Patient: Probably, my elder sister will take my jewellery and my savings will be used for paying for my brother's marriage, and the rest will be donated to a missionary post in Nigeria.

Because she begrudged her family in this prediction, she agreed she would bring her jewellery to her girlfriend and then donate her savings to a lesbian organization before committing suicide. My hope was that her girlfriend would ask the reason for the gift, resulting in her asking the patient to refrain from committing suicide. Fortunately, this happened. They both made an appointment for further help.

Case vignette: Finding good shelter for the surviving next of kin

After her husband's death, Mrs Brown, mother of two children, could not put her life back on the rails. Neither family or professional help, nor meditation and other spiritual activities could give her a reason for living on. She wanted to end her life, but not before having organized proper shelter for her children. Because of fear of involuntary admission and my reputation for applying admission-preventive strategies, she approached me to find such shelter (Jenner, 1984). Her conviction that her children would understand her remained immovable despite my strong conviction of the reverse.

She agreed to active searching for the best foster home, tailored to the needs of her children. My reasons behind this strategy were that: (1) it changed her focus of attention from the deceased husband to her children, (2) this search might possibly compel her to contact family and friends, and (3) she might discover that 'east, west, home's best'. My hope came true. Gradually the sense that her children needed her returned, together with joy for living and her zest for life.

Stage 6: Assessing the intention to die

The leading question reads 'Do you want to die, or are you desperate, unsuccessfully trying to solve your problems?' Most suicidal persons do not want to die, they only want to get rid of problems. This position is made pivotal. Next, therapy focuses on how to prevent a premature death.

Stage 7: Premature-death prevention agreement

A premature-death prevention agreement is made with the following text:

> I (name of the suicidal person) will actively work on my life for the following . . . days/weeks together with (name of) my therapist. I will respect my life. I'll try to the best of my abilities to prevent suicide during this period.

> In case I wish to break this agreement I will contact my therapist for discussing my wish. In case of his absence, I'll contact one of his substitutes. (Name of the therapist) commits on always informing his substitutes properly, and passing on their names and telephone numbers.

> Signed   Signed

> Name of the patient   Name of the therapist

Stage 8: Guidance about possible problems

Anticipatory guidance is given concerning how to deal with overwhelming emotions, possible conflicts and problems in performing coping strategies.

Stage 9: Next appointment

The next appointment is preferably given a bit earlier than the suicidal person considers to be necessary. This may help to optimize continuity of care.

HIT and traumatized patients

Relationships between a number of traumatic experiences and AVHs have been found. However, 83% of traumatized persons reported no voice hearing against 75% of voice hearers reporting traumatic experiences. Except for sexual trauma, my group found no significant relationship between trauma and voice hearing (Jenner *et al.*, submitted). In any case assessment of trauma is needed and treatment should be tailored to the person, AVHs and trauma in the case of traumatic experiences. HIT implements some of the following interventions: ego-strengthening, psychoeducation on and release of guilt feelings, linking voices and trauma, rituals such as the three-letter ritual written to the culprit, restoring social contacts, decision-making about yes/no judicial steps, crisis intervention and medication.

Case vignette: Clarice

This 16-year-old girl was sexually assaulted by four boys 14 months ago. They tore her clothes, but stopped and ran away when other people came by. This probably prevented her from being raped. Ever since, she hears voices calling her a whore, and threatening to rape her. This is a clear case of PTSD. In consultation with her parents, she decided not to take judicial steps. Voice monitoring reduced the frequency by about 30%. This gain made her less anxious and increased her hope for positive treatment results. Next, she improved on EMDR, but some voices remained. The remaining voices disappeared with a coping strategy of singing hymns and lecturing the voices on respect. Therapy was stopped after some ego-strengthening sessions. Full therapy took 10 sessions over a period of seven months.

Case vignette: Susan

For the last three days the patient (aged 21 years) had been unable to walk. No physical pathology was found. Some weeks ago she had started experiencing AVHs. Her case was urgent. In the reception hall her aunt and a sturdy tattooed man, her aunt's friend, supported a skinny young woman hanging in between them. They cared for her because her mother could not.

Information was heteroanamnestic because the patient did not reply to questions or just childishly replied: 'is good'. Her aunt was clearly in charge, with the patient utterly dependent on her. This did not appear to be episode dependent, but the regular situation.

At school Susan had been bullied, her intellectual capacities were limited, she could only work in protective, sheltered jobs. This was her third episode of AVH and somatoform (conversion) disorder. Episodes seemed to be related to both the sexual demands of her boyfriend, humiliation by her parents and being bullied at school.

Voices assessment: the voices appeared to be in power, frightened her and were commanding. She wished to regain control.

First, the lead of conversion was chosen. In line, her suggestibility was tested, which appeared fairly high. Next we assessed the patient's dependency. She started crying when we asked her family to leave the room for some time. We then asked her whether she considered her AVHs being of people who speak childishly. She denied this. Then we asked her to value the idea of showing her voices that she now had decided to regain control and as first step demonstrate this by starting to talk normally. Normal speech returned after coaxing and selective reinforcement. Next, she was advised to ask her aunt to leave the room as a sign of her new willpower. She did so after some coaxing. Each successful attempt was reinforced. Further, she was helped to demonstrate the voices her new willpower by standing upright without physical support. Finally, she invited her aunt and friend to rejoin the session. Their admiration boosted her self-confidence. In line, she was given three homework tasks: First, she was instructed to warn her voices by saying 'Today you have noticed my power, you better respect me and if not I'll use my power against you'. Her second task was voice monitoring (Appendix 4). The family was instructed about selective reinforcement and monitoring when they noticed the patient hearing voices. Her third task was to fill out TRAMAL (Appendix 5), a self-report list on traumatic experiences.

At second session voices had diminished, although selective reinforcement by the family had been counterproductive. In this session, psychoeducation on selective reinforcement and constructing a coping strategy was pivotal. Given her traumatic sexual relationship some individual sessions on sexual psychoeducation were given.

By the third session, the conversion paralysis and voices had completely disappeared. Sexual education was started by a female therapist. About the fifth session her comorbid anxiety disorder came into the open. She could be successfully referred to an anxiety therapy outpatient group. Treatment could be stopped successfully after nine months.

The successes described above are not representative. Complete disappearance of voices with HIT occurs in adolescents in about 65%, and in 20% of adult chronic voice hearers (Jenner and van de Willige, 2001; Jenner *et al.*, 1998, 2006b). Another 50% of the latter group improves in terms of reduced frequency, intensity, improved quality of life and social functioning. Quick successes in adult chronic voice hearers are rare. The mean duration of therapy in adult chronic patients is about nine months, with exceptions up to 3 years. However, a mean duration of five sessions is the rule in AUDITO, my children's voice-hearing outpatient department.

The following cases illustrate the complexity of treatment, especially when patients live in sheltered homes or are admitted to clinical units, where the patient system includes mental health-care workers who are familiar with applying other treatment styles. Because they sometimes experience HIT as strange, or even threatening, some HIT elements may need adjustment, and motivational strategies need to be tailored to the rules of the referring institutions. On the other hand, the willingness of staff to adjust to HIT and some flexibility of institutional rules are mandatory to guarantee the essentials of HIT. If these two conditions are absent, it may be better not to use HIT for the sake of the patient, who may get stuck.

Case vignette: Annie

For the last 15 years, Annie (aged 48 years) had alternated between sheltered homes and psychiatric admissions. Her psychiatric history started at the age of 12 after having been incestuously victimized by her father for over 6 years. Her marriage was just a flight from home, not for love. Her husband started sexual abuse in the second year of their marriage. Divorce occurred 9 years later. She was referred to the Voices Outpatient Department because of therapy-resistant suicide attempts due to voices that commanded her to commit suicide. I accepted referral on the following conditions: cooperation of her regular therapist in HIT, and active participation of ward staff in monitoring and implementing HIT interventions.

At the first session, the AVHRS assessment was an eye-opener for both patient, her therapist and her case manager. Annie's knowledge was restricted to the severity of her voices. Questions about number, frequency, loudness and control amazed her as well as her therapist. Psychoeducation about coping strategies and the effectiveness of HIT-induced hope. Homework tasks were: monitor your voices (Appendix 4), and have staff monitoring your behaviour and their reactions.

At the next session, it was found that Annie had monitored her voices irregularly. They were too many to monitor all. Hence, we adjusted the monitoring to only monitoring voices with intensity >7. She heard three types of voices: crying children, threatening male voices that commanded her to automutilate and attempt suicide, and a bunch of accusing, blaming and confusing voices. The children's voices saddened her and reminded her of the abortions her father forced her to undergo. The male voices threatened her with death, and the other voices confused her. Unfortunately, but consistent with our experience with mental health institutions, staff had not monitored at all. When asked about this it emerged that although they had said yes they did differently. Staff reacted inconsistently, with no selective reinforcement and an emphasis on punishment. These are conditions that are more disastrous than saying yes and doing nothing. Staff had omitted both monitoring for behaviour suggestive of AVH and positive reinforcement. These were clear indications of a divided staff.

The HIT strategy in such cases is as follows: on the first occasion of non-performance, we assume that we may have been unclear in our explanations. Hence, we repeat explanations and agreement. In the case of repetition, the next appointment is made dependent on the implementation of monitoring and HIT interventions.

We explained this strategy to the patient's regular therapist and case manager. At the third appointment again there had been no full staff monitoring. A new appointment was made dependent on two weeks of staff monitoring.

Four weeks later, the case manager called for a new appointment. He reported that monitoring had been completed for two weeks.

It was observed that staff interpreted odd behaviours as voice related. This interpretation appeared incorrect. More than 50% of incidents were related to conflicts with staff, irritations on the ward and problems at the sheltered workshop. We encounter this misinterpretation frequently in both relatives and therapists.

It was also found that staff selectively reinforced AVHs instead of reinforcing Annie's coping with voices. Staff were next instructed to do two things. First they should ask the patient: 'Do you hear voices?'. If she answers in the affirmative they then instruct her to start her coping programme. If not, they should ask her to behave normally. Secondly, they should reinforce her *after* she has applied the coping strategy, not before.

The patient chose to start coping with the children's voices. As the most likely explanation of these voices she decided that the children might be alter-egos representing her loneliness, confronting her with guilt feelings, and representing her need for love. Her coping strategy was constructed in line with this explanation: each time she heard the children she would sing children's songs and lullabies for 3 minutes. If there was significant reduction of intensity she might stop this coping. If not, she would start

(continued)

(continued)

redemption of her guilt feelings for 5 minutes by telling her alter-egos what had happened. If this did not give sufficient reduction of intensity she would walk for 15 minutes.

There are several reasons for this strategy. Singing lullabies is a logical activity in soothing children. Also, singing may interrupt the inner-speech loop, and may calm her and reduce her guilt feelings. The latter may also occur through the second coping behaviour. Please be careful when advising aggressive coping strategies when voice hearers relate voices to themselves. I strongly advise against their application because in such cases the aggression is indirectly aimed towards the voice hearer. This may enhance guilt feeling, induce hopelessness and depression, and may lower self-esteem.

With regard to suicidal ideation and automutilation, the patient was asked whether she liked her rapists to remain in command or whether she preferred taking over. For latter choice, the following coping strategy was suggested. Step 1: Tell your voice: 'You have ruined my life once. This time I am in command and I will stay alive at least until I have done with you' (3 minutes). Step 2: Sing a battle song (5 minutes). Step 3: Physical exercises (15 minutes).

Because this strategy may release severe emotions it has to be done in the presence of staff. The accompanying therapist and case manager were told not to allow the patient to start this strategy before staff had agreed to full cooperation. This programme needs a proper introduction because it terrifies most voice hearers. The patient is invited first to role play in the therapy room. The words need to sound decisive (even if the patient does not feel decisive) and convincing. Some practice may be needed. A number of female rape victims are obese, hence the physical exercises serve two goals at once.

Over the next six months Annie's coping with the children's voices improved. Guilt feelings about abortions disappeared, and her fury against the male voices increased. Three male voices belonged to rapists: her father, a nephew and a former boyfriend. Bargaining with third category voices reduced these to less than one hour a day. Her social functioning improved at the same time. However, neither anxiety management nor distraction helped against the rapists' voices. It was time to introduce venting off aggressive emotions.

Annie selected kicking a cushion each morning as her preventive activity, as well as any time she heard her male voices. At first she needed pushing to stick to the programme and the physical presence of staff. Eventually, she could cope with all the male voices except her father's.

Imaginary venting off of aggressive emotions is meant to give emotions elbow-room when aggression cannot be targeted to the person concerned because that person is too strong, feared or absent. Also, it protects the aggressor from damaging themselves and penal offence. It can be practised at any time, even in the absence of the person concerned. This brings the patient in control and gives him or her power, which is ego-strengthening. The venting is best practised in a ritualistic manner. One may choose between shouting all kind of curses to the (formerly) traumatizing person, beating and kicking a cushion or boxing ball, preferably with the perpetrator's name embroidered on it, throwing darts at the person's photograph or sticking needles in a puppet representing the culprit.

After 14 months of treatment, Annie had reached an acceptable status quo without suicidal ideation. Sporadic automutilation and third category voices still occurred, but her father's voice continued his threatening. During the next five months change stagnated so I gave her choice to either stop HIT or start evoking the remaining voices, focusing on her father's. Psychoeducation about the possible risks was discussed at length. Decision-making took her three months. Unfortunately, her sheltered home psychiatrist forbade her to evoke the voices. Therefore, transfer to the psychosis ward of the university hospital was needed. This ward focused on medication without experience in HIT. Nonetheless, these problems and the patient's exceptional status could be tackled and the patient was admitted.

The next stage started with the three-letters ritual. Many incest victims have ambivalent feelings towards the person who committed incest: on the one hand they are family, on the other they are the enemy; on the one hand they were seemingly treated as the favourite, on the other hand they were abused and threatened.

The three-letters ritual helps to separate these mixed feelings. Because emotions are pivotal, the focus should be more on emotions than on historical facts. The patient is told to write three letters. The first letter is intended to express negative experiences such as fury, aggression for reasons of abuse, humiliation and a ruined future. The second is about positive feelings such as affection, care and love. In the third letter both types of emotion find their appropriate places. This ritual may evoke violent emotions. Hence, proper arrangements need to be made and precautions taken. Contacts need to be frequent and a 24/7 crisis service arranged. In addition, the place and duration of writing should be agreed upon. Preferably, a quiet place should be provided with just a table, chair, pencils and a notebook, and as little distraction as possible. The use of bedrooms is strongly advised against for two reasons. First, bedrooms may be associated with incest. Second, the ritual may evoke emotions that disturb a night's rest. At the end, the final destination of the letters is discussed. Are they to be sent by post, personally delivered or ritually destroyed?

Annie's first letter was anything but emotional. Detailed questioning evoked severe emotions and she entered a state of dissociation. She agreed to active surveillance and support, was put under intensive observation, and had daily therapeutic sessions in this period. Stability returned after three months. However, the voices were as before. Four months later the three-letters ritual could be finished. Then it was time to change to evocation of voices.

Unlike anxiety management and distraction, the first evocation of voices session must be held in the presence of the therapist.

Annie dissociated in the first evocation session, which took well over 2 hours. In the subsequent discussion she was depressed, and feared that her father had won. His abusive and threatening voices were relabelled as the first signs of listening to her. His threatening was probably the last convulsions of a man who anticipates his defeat and of her becoming in command. The next session was programmed next morning. Gradually, she regained control. The voices became less frequent and less vehement, but remained. However, she could manage them.

The last period of therapy addressed her addiction to medication. This took half a year, and included suicidal ideation, threats of suicidal attempts and running away. Suicidal ideation returned to such an extent that a non-suicide agreement was needed (see paragraph above). The severity of signs and return of command AVH necessitated a protection plan. She was given the choice between locking the ward or being committed involuntarily. For locked doors she needed the permission of the other patients in her 'open' ward. She chose the first option and recovered in the next six weeks.

Eventually Annie was discharged from hospital. She was able to cope with her infrequent AVHs at a sheltered home for some years. Her last years she lived on her own with occasional help. She did not relapse till her natural death. All together, freeing her from AVHs and sheltered living took about 4 years.

Case vignette: Martin

Martin, 57 years of age, visited the Voices Outpatients Clinic in wintertime in shorts. He was referred as: 'Psychotic man who causes social agitation accusing his neighbours of harming and slandering for reason of talking in his head even in the middle of the night, and reading his mind'. His complaints were that neither had the police dealt seriously with his reports, nor had his accusations made the neighbours stop. Even his physical assaults had not worked. He became convinced that his neighbours were conspiring against him. He wanted me to convince the police of the mental disturbance of his neighbours.

His symptoms and behaviour made him a clear-cut paranoid psychotic patient. He also had a paranoid reaction to my psychiatric interview. It appeared that he had been homeless for the last 23 years. Before that, he had practised physiotherapy and been an active member of the Rotary Club and played sports. His breakdown occurred suddenly after his divorce. Recently, he had returned home to restore contact with his son, who refused to meet him. He lived on health insurance money. Communication was severely hampered by his idiopathic language and interminable deluded digressions. His preferred contact frequency was: 'I come when it suits me'. He argued that he was too busy for regular visits, but could not tell me what he was busy with. Once every six weeks was the final deal.

He appeared to be anorexic but refused physical examination, lab tests as well as any medication. He denied any illness because of his healthy food, which appeared to be one tin of beans daily. AVHRS assessment took 6 hours (the average time is 0.5–2 hours), and even then many items could not be scored reliably.

Having been told that the police need hard data he seemed eager to monitor his hallucinations, but time after time he failed to monitor what was mutually agreed upon. Lack of understanding seemed a major problem. I seriously considered stopping HIT treatment and referring the patient to neurology or the psychosis department. *Which decision would you take?*

Was the patient's non-compliance due to cognitive disability (he rejected psychological testing for delusional reasons) or was it resistance? Was it an autistic trait or brain damage? Should we put on pressure or stop treatment because of non-cooperation? The HIT team decided to give him the benefit of doubt, and to continue treatment.

At the 13th month we gave him three more months to find a way to start therapy. If not, we would stop. Finally, a golf counter and a chess clock

(continued)

(continued)

brought relief. Voices were counted, and voice periods clocked: the voices lasted more than 20 minutes/hour, 10 hours/day.

Coping training was then introduced, but rejected. It was not him but the neighbours. Because of his former musical interest he agreed to singing. His coping was successful: the voices disappeared during singing. Unfortunately, he did not continue to sing, but began to play the trumpet, which led to police interventions because of the noise at 2 a.m. Only a horror story about police intervention made him change his behaviour. The solution was membership of a local philharmonic orchestra, which had dual benefits: the frequency and duration of voices became less and social contacts increased.

About 17 months later, real change could be noticed. Martin allowed us to contact his sister. The impact of her involvement was great. She could restore contact with his ex-wife and their son. Social contacts ran parallel with decreased delusional thinking. Five months later, he appeared in a stylish suit and was playing sports again with his old teammates. The next year he was seen infrequently and therapy could be ended.

All together, this was a long therapy full of doubts and unclear decision-making. How and why his improvement occurred remains unclear, as is HIT's role.

The next case vignette demonstrates the sometimes bizarre and dangerous case of command hallucinations. It also illuminates the subtlety of words and counter-transference as well as the need to tailor an individual coping strategy and a safety environment.

Case vignette: Barbara

Barbara (aged 49 years) was referred because of therapy-refractory voices that commanded her to swallow 1–3 forks a week (forking). She was discharged from psychiatric hospital against her will because of 'forking' during admission. Her psychiatric history started at age 19. She is an incest victim; her father started abusing her at the age of 7. Her father (now deceased) had always denied the incest and her mother believed him and accused Barbara of lying. To get away from home, Barbara married. Her husband was (and is) respectable and respects her. They have two children. About 5 years ago she told her husband about her incestuous past.

Barbara's emergency admissions in general hospitals because of 'forking' were many times her 10 psychiatric admissions, three of which were non-voluntary. Admissions did not stop her 'forking'. DSM codes varied from psychosis, chronic depression to histrionic and borderline personality disorder. Incest was not mentioned in her files at the time of referral, it only became clear after some HIT contacts, at filling out the TRAMAL and the SPITE (Appendix 6).

Barbara and her husband were invited for an initial getting to know you session, with an introduction in HIT and risk assessment. She moved robot-like, showed hardly any expression and answered questions mechanically. Most of time her husband spoke. He sat quietly, looking sad and desperate. There was great discrepancy between her verbally expressed burden and her body language. She denied any control of 'forking' and her AVHs. She was told that the present risk of dying from 'forking' was too great for treatment at home. Ambulatory HIT could be started only after her being able to control 'forking' for at least two months. She was promised an appointment the day after. She and her husband were advised to monitor the voices. He called exactly two months later. Neither swallowing nor monitoring had occurred. I asked them to monitor AVH for one week and send me the files. They did so.

At the first session, AVHRS assessment was done. There were more than five voices, two men and three women. There were only negative abusing voices calling her a whore, predicting her gruesome death, and two commanding voices. Frequency was high, and possibly related to unexpressed irritation, which she denied. The burden on the family was severe and the voices were pivotal in almost all family life. Monitoring showed the voices' frequency and intensity to be related to the patient's level of activity. The couple strongly doubted this relationship. I agreed that the relationship might be coincidental and assessed her past. Her only two voice-free periods appeared related to activities too.

As motivating strategy we decided not to confront, but to apply directive questioning expressed in terms that were difficult to refuse. Also, the wording was directed to accepting the indirectly suggested homework task.

Our psychoeducation emphasized that activities (i.e. distraction) may lower voice burden. We also suggested that activities could be forms of showing the voices her wish to return to power. Finally, we asked her: 'You attribute your commanding voices great, real power. Do you expect powerful people to be more impressed by submissive, expectant and obedient

(continued)

(continued)

patients than by active, decisive ones? What do you think or, better, what do you want: to take action or to continue being the victim, showing your power or accepting their control?' Fortunately, she chose the active role, which we positively reinforced as a power act. She decided to become an attendant in a geriatric home as volunteer. It then appeared that her father had forbidden her to do a nursing course in the past. Barbara doubted that there was a relationship between this period and the beginning of the AVHs. She reported remembering voices before adolescence. Gradually, she worked four mornings a week with pleasure, and got good references. After a nine-month fork-free period treatment was ended. The patient still heard voices, but reported that she could handle them. At discharge her looks, emotions and movements had changed to normal.

Six months later, liaison psychiatry contacted us to refer a patient who was admitted at emergency for 'forking'. Barbara's voices and 'forking' had relapsed after four months. Shame had prevented her from asking our help.

The HIT programme was restarted. First, the past months were assessed. She had stopped her volunteer work. She had performed so well that the head of the unit had requested her to extend her work to three full days a week and offered her a permanent appointment. The voices had mocked her fear of responsibilities and inability to communicate this fear. 'Forking' started shortly after. She had not told her husband about her relapse. The emergency room's call had surprised him, and his anger was evident. We discussed the usefulness of telling and talking with her husband. Next, positive experiences and coping strategies were listed. At the same time as the increased stress she had stopped her coping programme. She restarted her last coping programme and asked her husband for support in implementation. At that time, trauma was assessed with the newly made TRAMAL. She heard her father's voice. He invited her to join him like before. This referred to his incest with Barbara and was indirectly an invitation to commit suicide because he had died. After an explanation of the three-letters ritual, she agreed to try it.

Although she agreed to this, the next week she 'forked' again without telling her husband. It remained unclear whether revenge, shame, stubbornness, fear of his anger or dissociation was a causal factor. Barbara said she did not know. In the following weeks, the frequency of 'forking' increased to several times a week. An emergency conference was convened with the patient, her husband, their son, the medical emergency team, the liaison psychiatrist, family doctor and me, with the focus on serious death risk. The patient emphasized both the absence of a death wish and her inability to resist the commands. Hence, I suggested admission on the psychosis ward, on condition of the staff's approval.

The ward accepted admission under strict conditions with penalty of discharge or referral to a closed ward. They also demanded that the HIT team take full responsibility. The nurses reported that the patient was negligent in complying with her coping plan. She said that fear of her father's power prevented her from implementing the three-letters ritual.

Our dilemma was as follows: Is this delusional, stubbornness, fear or exploring the boundaries? The patient was offered the presence of a nurse during writing. This is both real support in cases of fear, and controlled her writing. The 'forking' stopped, and gradually the patient overcame her fear.

Then, a case conference was held to generate extra alternative interventions. The staff questioned the HIT strategy, but offered no alternatives. Unfortunately, I had to stop the conference when the patient was questioned aggressively and indirectly accused by the audience. When questioned about being able to resist swallowing plastic forks, but not metal forks, Barbara reacted confused. When asked whether she realized that plastic forks break easily and may then be more dangerous than metal ones her husband reacted angrily. Next, one staff member lectured the patient for showing insufficient consideration of her husband and son and blamed her for selfishness. That same night the patient had to be admitted to casualty because she had swallowed plastic forks. She explained she had felt humiliated just as by her father in the past. She had become both angry and hopeless.

Making use of these emotions, the programme was adjusted to her strong ambivalence towards her father. The patient was instructed to record the present experiences and associations instead of rehearsing past memories. More emphasis was given to asking her father about the incest and telling him about her confusing emotions of both love and feeling abused. Also, she asked him for advice, and to accept her adulthood by changing his abusive style into an accepting and advising one. Change occurred. This new way of approaching her father suited her better. She constructed new ideas about him and his voices. At her discharge she hardly heard his voice. Occasionally she heard him murmuring what was interpreted as a kind of approval. In summary, the hallucinations remained, but could be fairly well handled with coping strategies. Other improvements continued too, and social activities increased as the family told me at my university farewell reception many years later.

The next case vignette is striking for several reasons. First, because it was not the voice hearer who was referred, but her 6-year-old son. Other differences were the bizarre commanding hallucinations and the actual continuation of trauma and threat that obstructed therapy.

Case vignette: Jamie

Jamie was referred for his aggressive unmanageable behaviour. His mother was unmarried. She had attended mediation and Gordon training. She was a feisty woman, impertinent, ostensibly open, but in fact defensive. She was also very suspicious, not least of social and mental health-care workers. She had a history of juvenile homes and pilfering.

A remarkable repeating pattern developed. Time and again, Jamie's mother's ever changing excuses inserted doubt about the real reasons behind her inconsistency in performing the advised actions. Her voices, visions and olfactory hallucinations came to the open when she asked advice about how to handle her son's sexually deviant behaviour. Central to her reports were family and unknown males entering the house. Asked about how they could enter without her permission it became clear that incest still occurred with her father and brother. Her parents forced her into prostitution, organized her clients and took the money. They had done so since her early childhood (confirmed by police reports). Her voices and olfactory hallucinations were related to this situation. She recognized her parents' voices and heard men screaming and scolding her.

Coping plans for this situation were far from effective. Voice monitoring remained incomplete despite a bunch of motivational interventions. It was decided the only way forward was to adjust the HIT approach to this odd and sad situation. Coping training was started, despite her inconsistent attitude and approach. When clients approached her son, I posed questions about her priorities: Was she prioritizing her work, her client, or her son's safety? She chose her son. Then I discussed possibilities for guaranteeing his safety. Scheduling client visits for when her son was sleeping over at a friend's home gave rest and protection. It took her three months to persuade her father to never again give clients the key to her house. At this point her nightly visions disappeared.

Singing seemed ineffective until we found that she listened to music rather than singing. Christmas songs whenever she felt sad or alone or hard metal whenever she felt angry helped in reducing the voices. However, this only lasted until the next setback. Then, procedures had to start again. Also, singing had no effect on her hallucinated father's voice.

Coping plans about his voice and quitting prostitution foundered on her fear of his revenge, which was realistic. In the past, he had discovered the address of the refuge where she lived and caught her, breaking her arm when she tried to escape.

Legal documents corroborated her story and the probable involvement of some policemen. Her fear made her decide not to try again to escape her father. Continuity of care and support was arranged, but HIT was stopped.

Case vignette: Cassie

The last case is Cassie, a young woman, 28 years of age, single and living in her parental home. For the last nine months she had been admitted to a closed ward of a mental hospital. She had severe aggressive outbursts in dissociative states. Treatment resistance and her parents' discontent with treatment had resulted in a transfer to the university psychiatric department. Here too her physically aggressive outbursts continued. Because of her AVHs and visual hallucinations the HIT team was called in for consultation.

Reports of Cassie's physical aggression led us to choose to see her with two therapists. In the beginning she was cooperative. Suddenly, when asked about traumatic experiences she dissociated: she rolled her eyes, stepped out of contact and physically attacked the co-therapist. We could overcome her attack and bring her back to reality with hypnotic suggestions. She looked around in a daze, and could not remember her dissociative period. We decided to give her the lead, and asked her whether she wanted information about what had happened, some rest, to return to the ward, or to continue. Our questioning was certainly suggestive towards the latter choice. In discussing the period preceding her dissociation she could remember some triggering items as well as physical sensations. These were enlisted as early warning signs. Repeating the session, she was able to caution, the session was stopped for some time and we continued again. This time no assault occurred, which gave her an ego-boost and some trust in HIT as well as in the feasibility of self-control. After finishing the regular HIT programme, an outpatient multi-family HIT aftercare programme could be completed.

Let us now focus on an ego-strengthening method. The regenerating and restoring powers of nature are great. However, severe and repetitive traumatic experiences take their toll, particularly in damaging ego functions and self-confidence.

There are many methods for strengthening self-confidence. In the context of these case vignettes counter-conditioning has been frequently applied.

- Step 1: Ask the patient to write as many positive characteristics about themselves as possible on cards: traits, skills, thoughts, feelings, activities, etc. In the case of a meagre list, ask key figures to contribute. Still a meagre list? First, ask for negative characteristics. Then ask: are you responsible for these negative characteristics, are you to be blamed for it, have you bad intentions? Ask whether other persons agree with the patient. If not, ask why he or she does not believe them? Second, neutralize and relabel. For example, a timid, silent person may call themselves a real bore. That may be true, but they are more than that. After all, thanks to the silent person, the narrator can shine. Do still waters not run deep?
- Step 2: The patient makes a stock of the cards, one card for each positive characteristic, preferably with special cards in their preferred colour. Sometimes one may ask a partner or relative to make the set of cards as signs of love, appreciation and support. With each bout of self-reproach, each degrading comment of voices, the voice hearer shuffles the stock, takes the topmost card and reads it aloud. The authenticity of the performance is important. If this does not convince outsiders, effectiveness cannot be expected. In such cases exercises in front of a mirror, the therapist or a relative can be recommended.
- Step 3: Finally, self-reinforcement and rewards from relatives are important. Another version of counter-conditioning is to evoke old positive memories of successful actions. This can be done with the hypnotherapeutic 'clenched fist' method. In this method the patient is invited and stimulated by suggestive questioning to re-experience positive past experiences. Hereafter, repetition is coupled to the gradual clenching of a fist. In a trance state the patient is told that simultaneously with fist-clenching the experiences become clearer and more vivid. Rehearsing this procedure may lead to re-evocation of positive feelings by just clenching the fist. Be aware that testing hypnotizability is an essential precondition. Also, hypnosis may be contraindicated in some traumatized patients who may feel overwhelmed and out of control in a hypnotic trance.

HIT adjusted for the intellectually disabled

It has been found that intellectually disabled voice hearers may benefit from HIT provided there are some adjustments. Common adjustments are: (a) simplify monitoring forms and cognitive interventions, (b) simplify and slow down speech and language, (c) emphasis on non-verbal interventions, (d) medication, (e) mediation, (f) operant conditioning, and (g) use of flashcards. Most of the time, various adjustments are needed in one therapy. The case above illustrated integration of some adjustments. Depending on the cognitive functions, participation of key figures is mandatory.

Simplify monitoring forms and cognitive interventions

Simplification can be achieved by reducing the number of monitoring items. For example, Date/What do voices say? (positive voices = smiley, etc.)/What have you done/did it work? (yes = +, no = –, and = means equal). If needed, restrict to just tallying or golf-ticker. Also, pictograms, colours, smileys instead of +/–, may be used.

Positive labelling and reframing are cognitive interventions that are both appreciated by and effective in intellectually disabled patients. As said before, these adjustments may help to create openness to change. In Peter's case (see earlier) labelling and reframing adjusted to his abilities resulted in fairly typical interventions. His voices were relabelled as a gift and his past history was reframed as horror in the form of psychoeducation.

Relabelling AVHs as a gift

Labelling AVHs as a gift – a cognitive intervention – may increase self-esteem, and also allows the voice hearer to appreciate his or her connected responsibilities. Peter's IQ score was 57. Labelling his delusion about being poisoned as a gift made him receptive for treatment that he had rejected earlier. Because of his strong rejection of any congruent approach focusing on insight, I switched to a hypercongruent approach and relabelled his delusion as a kind of talent or gift by comparing him with the Egyptian Pharaoh's food taster. This both chimed with his religious beliefs and delighted him, making him willing and able to replace his delusion-driven destructive behaviour with the more constructive view of protecting his parents.

Clear risk psychoeducation

Empathetic Socratic reasoning concerning the risk of civil commitment in reaction to possible aggressive outbursts in shops when confronted with 'poisoned' food on the shelves made Peter willing to take medication as part of his responsibility to protect his parents against poisoned food. As the reader will have noticed, the therapist switched from a congruent to a hypercongruent approach because of the patient's absolute rejection of the former approach. By this hypercongruent approach, the patient was made responsible for the consequences of his psychotic behaviour. This change implied a switch in focus from insight to behaviour and responsibility. This made sense because enduringly confronting severely deluded patients with their distorted reality testing may fortify their deluded conviction.

Simplification of language

This entails using simple words, short sentences, repetition and explicit control of understanding. Apply simple choices – yes/no, proposal 1 or 2 – and not too many at once. Slow down your speed. Make use of concrete, closed questions. I may ask whether they prefer white, if not, what about black, if not, what other colour? Be aware of socially desirable answers. Remember that choices may be influenced by framing and the order you present the choices: the last offered choice has the greatest chance of becoming accepted.

Emphasize non-verbal communication

Pictograms may work better than lectures. Reinforcement by relaxation, cuddling, touching, pictures, creative therapy, snoozing and so on are to be preferred over talking.

Mediation

Many intellectually disabled persons need the care of others, parents as well as professionals. Their involvement is mandatory because these patients need continuous support, control and help in understanding what is said. As the cases of this paragraph illustrate, treatment of moderately and more severely intellectually disabled patients is hardly possible without the involvement of key figures. Their involvement is necessary for getting the homework tasks implemented, as well as for operant conditioning and selective reinforcement, preferably contingently. Be alert to differences in reference and treatment style between HIT and institutional rules and regulations. For example, the directive HIT style may be incompatible with rigid permissive and incongruent intuitive emotional styles. Large differences may be a reason not to implement HIT. Another contraindication may be lack of staff.

Operant conditioning

Hearing voices is a double-edged sword: it is both disturbing and rewarding. Normally, the therapist spends more time on problematic than on normal behaviour. In other words the therapy may unknowingly reinforce problematic behaviour, including symptoms. Unfortunately, many relatives as well as mental health-care workers are not well informed about the rewarding side of symptoms that evoke reactions in others. Hence, psychoeducation about selective reinforcement is mandatory before a change can occur from rewarding (e.g. talking about) symptoms towards reinforcement of coping with symptoms and symptom-free behaviour. The effectiveness of operant conditioning with contingent tokens has been proved in intellectually disabled persons. In addition, the token economy has been developed for these patients. Patients may win tokens by cooperation and successes, and lose tokens when non-cooperative. Flashcards may be used as reinforcers, with x cards being changed for y favours. The choice of favours will depend on personal circumstances and preferences.

Case vignette: Adjusted flashcards

Fred (aged 23 years, IQ 66) had a long psychiatric history at his referral to the Voices Outpatients Department. For quite some years his voices had threatened him. They said: 'We will cause a psychotic relapse and commit rehospitalization when you don't obey us'. They commanded him to run away from home. He doubts the reality of the voices, but fears them to be right. His frustration due to the gap between his capacities and expectations may be causal.

First, the sequence of events, thoughts, feelings, behaviour and consequences is explained. Next, he is told that voices may be negative, positive, helpful and useful. Further, the possibility is raised that his voices intend to protect him against rehospitalization, but do this ineffectively and stupidly. They probably are a bit dumb. This terminology has been deliberately chosen because of the observed gap. We expected him to become more cooperative in beating dumb voices than clever ones. After he agreed to this proposition he was invited to reassure his voices that he had no plans to run away (self-suggestion). His case manager promised Fred he would resist civil commitment. Next, Fred was requested to evaluate his voices: Are they helpful? Are they reliable? If so, he would thank them and tell them that their help was no longer needed. If not, he would sing a battle song. His parents were involved as referees. Each time he made the right judgement his parents would give him a flashcard, and another one for each right reaction to the voices. His flashcards were comic characters, smileys and high-fives. Wrong evaluations were given supportive flashcards, stimulating another trial.

Case vignette: Integrated adjustments

A male patient, 51 years of age, IQ 45, diagnosed with the Prader–Willi syndrome (PWS), was referred because of imperative and restrictive AVHs. These had severe negative consequences for his quality of life and for that of his fellow residents at a sheltered home. The patient wanted to get rid of his voices.

His history mentioned repeated psychotic episodes, hallucinations and delusions of grandeur and religiosity; self-neglect; obsessive–compulsive disorder (washing, rituals); hyperphagia and obesity; dysmorphia and temper tantrums. He also had nephrogenic diabetes insipidus due to lithium. His present medication was olanzapine and valproic acid. The complexity

(continued)

(continued)

of this case, foster home and staffing made us accept the referral under strict conditions only.

Stage 1: Deliberations about accepting the referral

The active participation of the case manager and sheltered home staff was mandatory because of: (a) their expertise and experience with PWS, (b) the patient's rituals and temper tantrums, (c) the absolute need for consequent reinforcement, (d) patient safety, (e) reduction of stress, and (f) the transfer of HIT knowledge to the staff. The referents accepted these conditions and therapy was started.

Stage 2: Diagnostic session

The aims were observation of patient's behaviour, patient–staff interactions, effect of exploratory interventions, and AVHRS and PUVI assessment.

The patient was overactive, catching the attention of his counsellors. The counsellors tried to calm him down and reassure him. Escalation could only be stopped with stern words. The patient obsessively shook hands with me, moved his chair and questioned me. This could be stopped with a challenge about the minimum ritual time he could achieve: the patient reacted positively to this challenge and even succeeded in less time than he had bet. With positive rewards he became increasingly cooperative, much to the surprise of the staff.

AVH assessment was established with the help of his case manager. The patient heard negative voices of unknown origin. Some gave commands, most of which he could resist. Staff saw him talking to invisible subjects. He reacted obsessively when he did not understand the voices. The voices were in the second person, and had further characteristics he did not know. There were no delusions.

Staff reacted inconsistently and seemed to reinforce the wrong behaviour. Relabelling his voices as holy terrors pleased him. Enthusiastically he executed changing roles with the voices by lecturing them and calling them to order. Two coping strategies were suggested as homework: (1) sending away unwanted voices and (2) calling them to order. The patient beamed when complimented for his endeavour. He agreed to tally his exercises and their successes and tell staff the results of his coping exercises. Staff would reinforce his coping behaviour instead of his complaints about AVH. Staff were advised to prompt him to cope when he complained, instead of their usual understanding explanations and reassurance. The next session was planned after a fortnight.

Stage 3: Coping training

Operant conditioning of obsessive behaviour was repeated as in stage 2. We noticed that the case manager and staff had copied our behaviour with fairly good results. The patient was satisfied with the results of his coping programme. His coping was nearly always successful. Singing helped on the few occasions that sending away did not work. He no longer worried about the voices and felt strong. This was noticeable in his behaviour. Staff reported improvements in his AVH and social activities, and diminished obsessive–compulsive rituals and temper tantrums. All were reinforced extensively, a new session was planned one month later.

Stage 4: Concluding

The voices had hardly occurred and residual voices disappeared with coping. The patient felt relieved, and the results of treatment had improved his trust in the staff. Communication on the ward between patient, staff and other patients had improved too.

The patient died some years later, a natural death. Up till his death the improvements remained.

HIT for children and adolescents

Voice hearing and trauma in children and adolescents

The occurrence of hallucinations in children and adolescents is fairly high, especially of AVH followed by voice hearing combined with visions. Prevalence rates vary from 2 to 30% with a peak of 63% recorded in an American state hospital (Jaffe, 1966). The highest rates were found among psychiatrically disordered children. Population-based studies report that about 9% of children in middle childhood hear voices (Bartels-Velthuis et al., 2010; McGee et al., 2000; Yoshizumi et al., 2004). At a young age no gender difference has been found, but adolescent boys have a two times higher prevalence than girls, while the prevalence among adult women is twice the rate in men. Real prevalence rates are probably higher because hallucinations are regularly missed in children.

There is growing evidence of an association between childhood traumatic experiences, such as physical and sexual abuse, bereavement, separation and bullying, and hallucinations.

Auditory and visual hallucinations in non-clinical persons appear to be significantly related to adverse childhood events, rape, physical and sexual assault, but not to parental death (Goldstone *et al.*, 2012; Shevlin *et al.*, 2011). A dose–response effect of childhood adversity and AVH has been observed (Bentall *et al.*, 2012). In addition, childhood emotional trauma, combined with subsequent difficulties in life and stressful life events in a non-clinical sample were associated with vulnerability to AVH (Bartels-Velthuis *et al.*, 2011; Glaser *et al.*, 2010; Myin-Germeys *et al.*, 2005). In the study by Escher *et al.* (2002) over 75% reported one or more traumatic events around the time of voice onset. Childhood adversity was observed in a small group of children (mean age 12.9 years), whereas high scores on life events relating to the onset of AVH were observed in the entire group.

Bartels-Velthuis *et al.* (2012b) observed a significant association between social adversity level (both traumatic and stressful events were assessed) and AVH in their 5-year follow-up of a baseline case–control sample (*n* = 694) of 7- and 8-year-old children from the general population with and without AVH. Adolescents with a combination of AVH and delusions experienced significantly more traumatic and stressful events than those with either AVH or delusions alone. Persistent AVHs may occasionally occur, with a persistence rate ranging from 23.5 to 27%. The persistence rate was measured in the 5-year follow-up study in which (part of) the case–control sample (347 children with and 347 without AVH, at age 7 and 8) participated (Bartels-Velthuis *et al.*, 2012b). The number of voices, their frequency and negative tone, lower level of global functioning, comorbid psychopathology and use of cannabis have been found to be risk factors. AVHs that persist during adolescence indicated a five- to sixfold higher risk of developing psychosis (Welham *et al.*, 2009).

Fortunately, AVHs are transitory in most children of middle childhood (Bartels-Velthuis *et al.*, 2011). In the study by Escher (2004) 75% of voice-hearing children reported the experience of traumatic events or circumstances beyond their control. Over a period of 3 years the voices disappeared in 60% of the subjects. Lataster *et al.* (2006) found that both severe and mild traumatic experiences were associated with non-clinical psychotic symptoms.

In the study by Shevlin *et al.* (2008), physical abuse, neglect, rape and molestation were associated with visual hallucinations, and physical abuse, rape and molestation with tactile ones, while AVHs were associated with rape and molestation. Bartels-Velthuis *et al.* (2012b) found no such specific relation between AVH and type of traumatic experience. A positive association was found between severity of AVHs (measured with the AVHRS; Jenner and van de Willige, 2002) and the number of traumatic experiences. Adding up the persistence rates of the studies by Bartels-Velthuis *et al.* (2012b) and Escher *et al.* (2002), it can be concluded that over 6.5% of the adolescent population suffers from severe and persisting hallucinations.

In view of the high correlation with suicidal ideation (Kelleher *et al.*, 2010, 2011, 2012) and the risk of developing psychotic disorders in adolescence, in this group a preventive approach is warranted. In addition, better detection is mandatory, and stigmatization and self-fulling prophecies should be prevented. One may consider the following stepwise approach:

1   Start awareness programmes.
2   Train health-care professionals and school teachers to detect hallucinations.
3   Assess the severity of voices (>5 on the AVHRS severity score is a risk).
4   Psychoeducation, support and follow-up of latter group.
5   Therapy if needed.

Development-related models postulate associations between AVHs and disturbances in growth in pre-, peri-, postnatal periods and early childhood predictors of psychoses later in life. Research data on this subject are equivocal as yet. Cannon *et al.* (2002) found persisting early childhood disturbances in the development predisposing for psychotic-like symptoms in prepuberty and schizophrenia spectre disorders in adolescence and adulthood. The findings of the studies by Clarke *et al.* (2006) and Zammit *et al.* (2009) support this finding. In contrast, Bartels-Velthuis *et al.* (2010) could not find an association between AVHs and psychotic-like symptoms in their follow-up population study among 7- to 13-year-old children.

Several studies have found relations between non-clinical psychotic symptoms and growing up in urban areas (Spauwen *et al.*, 2006). Van Os *et al.* (2009) summarized evidence for this finding. However, in the study by Bartels-Velthuis *et al.* (2010) children in urban areas had less, but more intense AVHs than children from rural areas.

There is growing evidence that traumatic experiences at a young age put subjects at risk of developing psychiatric symptoms (Mackie *et al.*, 2011; Read *et al.*, 2001; Walker and DiFerio, 1997). Negative consequences of sexual harassment and bullying have been clearly shown. Lataster *et al.* (2006) found a clear-cut dose–effect relationship between non-clinical psychotic symptoms on the one hand and the other victims (odds ratio (OR) 4.8), and bullying (OR 2.9). The findings fit a more-track model of early defects, handicaps and trauma causing persistent stress. This stress leads to increased levels of glucocorticoids that permanently change the hypothalamic–pituitary–adrenal (HPA) axis. A change in the HPA axis results in increased dopamine levels (Walker and DiFerio, 1997). At the same time, negative life events make neurodevelopment more sensitive to stressors. This effect of negative life events is both age and frequency dependent (Garety *et al.*, 2001).

The majority of childhood hallucinations are transitory. However, the persistence found in about 40% of pre-adolescent children (Escher, 2004) is worrying. Nearly 25% of middle childhood children reported persistent voices at 5-year follow-up. The score on the primary school exit examinations of these children was significantly lower than scores for both non-hallucinating and transitory hallucinating children. Persistent AVH children also attended lower level secondary schools (Bartels-Velthuis *et al.*, 2012b). At 5-year follow-up another 9% reported AVHs. At highest risk was the combination of hallucinations and delusional thoughts.

HIT and suicidal ideation in children and adolescents

Definitions of suicidal behaviour as well as the discrimination between suicidal ideation, suicidal behaviour and risk of suicidal death colour the debate on suicide prevalence and suicidal risk. The development of a death concept is a three-stage process. In the first stage, children see death as temporary and reversible until their fifth year of age. The suicidal danger in this period is limited by the child's physical limitations. In between the 5th and 10th years personification of death occurs. It is better not speak to a child about an intention to die before the age of 10. Abstraction of death and a more adult death concept is the final stage. However, for some time the child's expectation continues that unrealizable wishes can be fulfilled after death.

Traumatic experiences in childhood and age of first suicide attempt are associated. Attempts before the age of 20 have a significantly higher childhood–age trauma score compared to first attempts at older age (Roy, 2004). The meaning of suicidal behaviour is age dependent. In children and pre-adolescents suicidal behaviour usually has no primary suicidal meaning. Death seldom is the final goal. At this age suicidal attempts are seldom calculated. They are not based on the ambivalence of life and death that characterizes an adult's attempts (Kienhorst et al., 1993). Suicidal behaviour in young adolescents is mainly impulsive, appealing and demonstration coloured (Atkinson et al., 2007; Hawton et al., 2003; Kandel et al., 1991).

It has been found that among students depression, drug abuse and eating disorder have the greatest predictive value for suicidal behaviour (Kienhorst et al., 1993). Automutilation and disturbed family relations were independent predictors in depressive adolescents. Clinically relevant is a person's intention to die. Suicidal death may be the result of both achieved suicide, and a suicidal attempt that got out of control. In contrast, survival may be the result of 'just' an attempt as well as a failed suicide. This distinction is badly missed in most studies. Recently, hallucinations and psychotic symptoms in general have been detected as important markers of risk for suicidal behaviour (Kelleher et al., 2012). This group discovered a 10-fold increased odds of any suicidal behaviour in early (OR 10.23; 95% confidence interval 3.25–32.26) and middle Irish adolescents (OR 10.54; 95% CI 3.14–35.17). Adolescents with depressive disorder and comorbid psychotic symptoms were at nearly 14-fold increased odds of more severe suicidal behaviour (plans as well as acts) compared with adolescents with depression only (OR 13.7; 95% CI 2.3–89.6). Adolescent suicidal ideators with comorbid psychotic symptoms had a nearly 20-fold increased odds of suicide plans and acts compared with suicidal ideation-only adolescents (OR 19.6; 95% CI 1.8–216.1).

Therapy for adolescents is identical to that for adults. Preventive actions are: (1) training parents, teachers and health-care staff in sensitivity for risk factors, (2) disconnect guilt (Western countries) and shame (Eastern countries) from suicidal behaviour, (3) media rules for reporting suicide, (4) self-reflection on standards and values regarding suicide. SEDAS (Semantic Differential Attitudes towards Suicidal behaviour; Jenner and Niesing, 2000) is a helpful instrument for making people aware of these hidden standards and values. SEDAS consists of 15 pairs of adjectives concerning suicidal behaviour and thoughts. The pairs describe feelings and opinions in the following actor/situation sets: own suicide, that of an adolescent, a middle-aged addict, an elderly person, someone with incurable tumour, and so on. The psychometrics of the instrument – internal consistency (values between 0.70 and 0.86), item–rest correlation (0.63) and test–retest correlation (0.87) – are acceptable to good. Trainees fill out their own judgement per pair and per situation. SEDAS is also helpful in estimating suicidal risk. Semantic differential scales have the property of being able to scale both the intensity and the direction, as is needed in judging suicide. SEDAS has also proved a useful instrument for training professionals.

Therapies for voice-hearing children and adolescents

Some case vignettes of voice-hearing children and adolescents have been described in other chapters. Here are two more cases and their therapies.

Case vignette: The detective game

Paul (aged 7 years) was referred for treatment-resistant voices. He has an autistic disorder and attention deficit hyperactivity disorder (ADHD). Social contacts and making friends were problematic. One year ago imperative voices had started. However, neither Paul nor his parents had informed me about his stealing behaviour. The family were his mother and father, sister Mette (8 years) and brother Brian (13 years). Paul had a pivotal position in his family. This became problematic when Brian moved to secondary school, one year ago. At this time the parents gave Brian a controlling role in preventing Paul's stealing behaviour.

Initially all three children denied stealing. Mother caught Paul by a trap. An interesting question became apparent with regard to the relationship between the stealing and the command hallucinations. The latter occurred *after* the first theft. Is there only a time connection? Is it an example of secondary gain? Is it determined lying? The latter cannot be excluded.

Paul gets a kick out of the suspense related to the stealing process. He buys 'friends' at school with stolen money. His parents disguised the thefts with the cloak of 'charity', neither raising the matter nor calling him to order. Paul expressed his regret, and promised to mend his ways. Increased

(continued)

(continued)

allowances meant to stop the stealing were in vain: the thefts continued. At the moment of punishment, Paul reported his imperative hallucinations. Then a few weeks ago, suicidal ideation appeared.

A systemic hypothesis is that the voices are functional and prevent punishment. They were probably absent at the beginning. Parental behaviour may have induced and reinforced the hallucinatory component. Brian's controlling task restricts his outgoing behaviour and related stress in the family. Stealing and suicidal ideation prompt the parents to frequent deliberations, which intensified their contacts.

For the HIT programme, the detective game was suggested with the following explanation. Paul has ADHD which means he is quickly bored, bringing him to excitement-seeking behaviour. Playing a detective may replace the thrill of stealing. Detective Paul is bound to inform the voices: 'From now on I am detective and can neither steal nor listen to you'. The parents will hide some money, the treasure, each day. Paul has to find the treasure within 15 minutes. If he succeeds, the money is put in the family treasure-chest, from which family trips may be funded. The parents act as game referees and determine the trips. Initially, the parents were reluctant but they agreed after psychoeducation on selective reinforcement and with the condition that the treasure money is always less than the sum stolen.

All will gain: the weekly treasure is less than the stolen sum. Brian can stop controlling Paul. The family gains too: going out together. Paul's excitement is guaranteed without stealing.

At the next session, the family reported enthusiastically about the detective game. Paul had successfully informed his voices, no money had been stolen and he had succeeded in finding the treasure three times in seven days. Suicidal ideation has gone. All looked forward to the first trip.

Three months and four mediation sessions later therapy could be stopped. Stealing, AVH and suicidal ideation had all stopped.

Comic strip writing/drawing may be used for children who have difficulties in verbal expression. After diagnostics have been concluded, this therapy may be suggested. The patient and therapist select a plot in turn. Then they draw pictures of the strip. This gives the therapist ample chances to steer, reinforce and restructure. Drawing gives a person the possibility of expressing emotions without the need for verbalization.

Case vignette: Strip drawing and writing

Theodore (aged 12 years) heard terrifying voices that frightened him so much that he did not dare to go upstairs in the dark to his bedroom. Neither play therapy, family treatment, medication, music therapy nor supportive therapy had helped. At referral, the family's expectations and motivation were low. Theodore's answers were evasive, until our shared interest in comic strips came into the open. That ended in a contract of drawing strips. Among his selected items were: destruction by space warriors, Superman against the villains, Ghostbusters against evil spirits, Donald Duck, bravery and love. His first strip ended sadly with the destruction of mankind except a few good men. This revealed his suicidal ideations. I just followed his mood in my drawings, adding word balloons with questions about how, when and where. He exposed a lot of hatred and revenge feelings. In turn I introduced Dombo the elephant, who turned into a cheerful artist despite having been bullied and ridiculed. Another time the friendly ghost Oscar was introduced. After each strip Theodore selected a hero. The next step was strips circling around evil spirits, ghosts, monsters and extraterrestrials. Time and again his heroes were introduced to find solutions, overcome problems and vanquish demons. Finally, we discussed his voices.

When coping strategies were introduced he was repeatedly asked which strategy his heroes would apply and how they would do it. He was then asked whether he could do it with the help and advice of his heroes. Suicidal ideation disappeared, and drawings were made of the results. By the fifth month he had overcome his voices and fears and was awarded a Ghostbusters' hero award signed by his parents and the therapist.

Part 4

Other hallucination-focused therapies

Chapter 6

Cognitive behaviour therapy for psychoses (CBTp)

The founding father of CBT, Aaron Beck, first introduced this treatment paradigm in a 1952 case study on therapy for a patient with chronic paranoia. Cognitive behaviour therapy for psychoses (CBTp) proposes that beliefs and behaviours, including deviant behaviour and psychotic symptoms, are to a certain extent learned and can be unlearned. Psychotic AVH is enabled by psychobiological vulnerability and neurotransmitter imbalance. However, it is the attribution of negative power to these voices, along with a lack of control and mastery, that discriminates voice hearers with and those without a psychiatric disorder (Romme *et al.*, 1992). Biases and false interpretations of the hallucinatory experience result in delusional thinking and anxious or depressive emotions. Avoidance behaviour reinforces secondary delusions that gradually functions as a narrative that controls the voice hearer's life. Antipsychotic medication hardly improves these secondary delusions.

CBTp applies the ABC postulate, where A stands for the Activating event (hallucination), B for a person's Belief about the event, and C for the emotional or behavioural Consequences that follow from these beliefs given the activating event (Chadwick and Birchwood, 1996). This framework assumes that problems are mainly related to A only in terms of Bs such as attributions of power to voices, feeling terrorized, and so on. The A factor (AVH) itself is assumed to be a minor factor relative to the B factor. Behavioural conditioning plays a large role; the shorter the contingency interval and the more inconsistent the C the stronger the B is being strengthened. The primary targets of CBTp are the interpretations of and attributions to AVH. The choice of these specific targets is supported by studies that have found less disastrous attributions being associated with better social functioning (Honig *et al.*, 1998).

Attributions of excessive power and malicious intent uniquely predict the presence of psychiatric disorders in voice hearers (Chadwick and Birchwood, 1994). Socratic questioning is a commonly used and powerful method for partly changing attributions because it avoids direct persuasion or accusations that the patient is wrong. The therapist instead helps patients to draw on their own experiences and doubts to discover that there are other ways of making sense of their experiences (Chadwick and Birchwood, 1996: 42).

Pivotal in CBTp is helping patients to re-attribute the relationship between their voices and the emotions they evoke. Self-instructions have proved to be effective instruments in this re-attribution. They help voices in becoming more internally generated. This helps to reduce the power formerly attributed to the voices, making them less frightening and more controllable. The characteristics of voices, such as frequency, duration, etc., are assessed and the ABC model is taught explicitly. Psychoeducation centres around the stress vulnerability hypothesis and psychotic reasoning processes.

According to van der Gaag (2012), the basic assumptions for changing the patient's attributions are fourfold: (1) Voices are disturbing symptoms of a disorder and are internally, not externally, generated. They are not expressions of hidden thoughts or wishes of the voice hearer. (2) Reduction of power attribution to voices. Their predictions are inaccurate, invalid or vague. Their threats are false. Hence there is no reason for avoidance or for following imperatives. (3) Voices have no meaning; they are no more than noise nuisance. Assumptions are that changing attributions in this direction will induce reduction of anxiety, depressive symptoms and desperation, and will increase control and feelings of mastery and self-competence. As a result, patients may have a better quality of life irrespective of their AVHs. (4) Change in attribution may improve control of negative emotional consequences of AVH. More detailed information on CBTp can be found in the review by Thomas et al. (2014).

Individual CBTp

Indications and contraindications for individual CBTp

There is a lack of research on indications and contraindications for CBTp. Generally speaking, low intelligence, severe disorganization and inadequate mastery of language are contraindications. The best outcomes have been reported among patients with persistent voices in the absence of disorganization. A meagre effect, if any, was found in patients absolutely convinced of their own judgement and lacking interest in the opinions of others (van der Gaag, 2012).

Scientific evidence for the effectiveness of individual CBTp

Several meta-analyses have been published on the effectiveness of CBTp (Cormac et al., 2002; NICE, 2011; Pilling et al., 2002; Thomas et al., 2014). Since 1952, a variety of CBT programmes has been created to such an extent that this development may endanger the validity of CBTp meta-analyses. For example, one NICE meta-analysis included HIT as a CBTp programme, which it is not. This variety in CBTp programmes may explain why CBTp effectiveness meta-analyses demonstrate variations in effect size from 0.25 to 0.47 (latest NICE study 0.30). Overall, there is evidence for beneficial but modest effects on positive symptoms (overall severity, voice-related distress, disability, compliance and voice frequency: Thomas *et al.*, 2014). Initially, impressive and enduring effects of CBTp on delusions were reported. At present this high effect is being doubted by some researchers. The effect on hallucinations exists, but is limited. In an RCT by Tarrier *et al.* (2004) the effects of CBTp did not significantly differ from those from TAU or supportive counselling. Kuipers *et al.* (1997) reported significant differences in favour of CBTp upon follow-up. However, their study demonstrated a dramatic site-of-treatment influence. Valmaggia *et al.* (2005) reported CBTp to be superior to TAU on frequency and loudness of voices, and on external attribution (NNT = 7). However, differences were no longer significant at six-month follow-up.

Results from a special CBTp programme for command hallucinations (Byrne, 2003) are very promising, especially for forensic patients. Although the frequency and impact of the voices did not change, patients' non-compliance with command hallucinations was substantially greater in the CBTp condition (86%) than in the control group (47%) (Trower *et al.*, 2004).

Group CBTp

Group treatment has both advantages and disadvantages compared to individual treatment. One justification for group treatment is that groups offer better opportunities for sharing experiences and mutual support than do individual settings. The presence of other voice hearers may help to lower the barrier of shame experienced by many people who do not dare to talk about their voices. In group therapy many voice hearers realize for the first time in their life that their experiences are not unique. Other advantages of group treatment include the facilitation of social contact, recognition of the stages of reaction to AVH, and an opportunity to test ideas about the power of the voices (Wykes *et al.*, 2005). According to Pennings and Romme (1997), peers facilitate the process of making sense of one's voices. Group members may make more acceptable role models than therapists, and people appear to be less likely to reject suggestions made by their peers than those made by therapists or relevant others (Steultjens, 2012). Patient self-expression, mutual support, sharing of experiences, a recognition of the effectiveness of coping strategies, similarities and differences in personal narratives and beliefs, are all pivotal in group treatment.

One disadvantage of group treatment is that it offers fewer opportunities to attend to individual symptoms and needs than do individual and systems treatment (Wykes *et al.*, 2005). Probably the greatest risk of a group model is the possibility of negative reinforcement due to stressful and emotional confrontations with the experiences of fellow sufferers. These confrontations may introduce the possibility of self-harm, suicide and the reliving of traumatic experiences, which can be demoralizing. Other risks imposed by the presence of group members include disrespectful behaviour, such as being overawed by symptoms, factitious mimicking of symptoms, and unrealistic feelings of responsibility for group members. Group treatment depends on a clear structure and a safe, reliable environment that maintains boundaries and nips peer pressure in the bud (Janzing, 1966).

Most group treatment programmes for voice hearers have a more or less standardized CBTp component. All models of group CBTp stress an acceptance of the reality of voice hearing, with realistic expectations as to the chances of complete recovery, and a reorientation of the patient's priorities towards the development of an adjusted attitude towards the voices. This reorientation is carried out by giving an alternative theoretical concept of the voices and by teaching effective coping strategies that will result in renewed mastery. Coping training may include negotiations with voices instead of fighting them, or labelling them as a kind of background noise with only a metaphorical speech content (Bach and Hayes, 2002). Other topics covered in group CBTp may include learned helplessness, independence, assertiveness and a consideration of the impact of AVH on interpersonal relations (Birchwood et al., 2002).

Group CBTp programmes vary widely in other aspects. They may differ in terms of inclusion criteria, number of sessions and duration of treatment. Some programmes may involve significant others. Most use homework while some do not. Programmes also vary in their explanations of AVH, especially with regard to its relationship with psychiatric disorders. Wykes' (2005) programme employs a biologically oriented concept of schizophrenia, while two programmes inspired by the Empowerment Movement (see below) disagree with this theoretical framework and treat AVH as secondary to traumatic events (Romme and Esher, 2012; Steultjens, 2012). These programmes also vary in duration of treatment (6–12 weekly sessions), duration of sessions (1–1.5 hours) and number of attendants (4–8). British studies typically apply the ABC model and include patients with schizophrenia only, while Dutch programmes apply a trauma-related causal model and include patients with dissociative disorder and borderline personality disorder as well.

Indications and contraindications for group CBTp

The indications and contraindications for group CBTp have yet to be determined. As yet, no research into the relative advantages of homogeneous versus heterogeneous diagnostic groups exists. Nevertheless, existing programmes have in common that participants must be able to follow group rules and respect the boundaries and opinions of others. Openly aggressive behaviour is an absolute contraindication. Relative contraindications are severe disorganization, restlessness and developmental disabilities.

Scientific evidence for the effectiveness of group CBTp

The effectiveness of group CBTp on AVH has been evaluated in studies using a naturalistic design (Chadwick et al., 2000b), a within-group design comparing waiting list patients with themselves during treatment (Wykes et al., 1999) and an RCT (Wykes et al., 2005).

The patients in Chadwick's group did not improve on anxiety, depression (as measured with the Hospital Anxiety and Depression Scale) or on characteristics of their voices (measured with the Hustig and Hafner rating scale). Significant improvements were measured in diminishing the power and omnipotence that voice hearers attributed to the voices (Chadwick *et al.*, 2000a). Satisfaction with this programme was high but with great individual variation. In Wykes' waiting list study, significant but short-lived improvements in symptoms were found with group CBTp as measured by the Brief Psychiatric Rating Scale. Significant and enduring improvements were found in some characteristics of patient's AVH as measured by the AHRS, and in self-esteem as measured by Rosenberg's Self-Esteem Scale. The authors measured significant and enduring improvements in insight as measured by the Insight for Psychosis Scale but not on the Beliefs About Voices Questionnaire. Application of coping strategies did not improve treatment results that varied widely per patient.

In the RCT, social functioning measured with the Social Behavior Schedule improved significantly more in the CBTp group than in the control group primarily due to improvements at follow-up. Characteristics of voices as measured by the AHRS hardly changed. Self-esteem and coping behaviours improved equally in both conditions. Newton *et al.* (2005) found similar results with Wykes' programme. Non-compliance rates have not yet been systematically examined.

In the group CBTp RCT by Penn *et al.* (2009) greater improvements on general psychopathology were found in the group CBTp condition than in the control group. However, in most respects the programme did not yield differential improvements for AVH. The control condition – supportive therapy for AVH – showed generally better and broader improvements in AVH than group CBTp.

Chapter 7

The Empowerment Movement

The Hearing Voices Movement began in 1986 in the Netherlands at a conference for voice hearers, their friends and family, and therapists (Romme and Esher, 1989). This movement stresses the importance of finding meaning in voices and in emancipating psychiatric patients. Pivotal empowerment-based interventions involve encouraging voice hearers to accept their voices and their ownership by studying their significance and origin, regaining power over AVH through personal coping styles, and supporting voice hearers in a process of transformation from psychiatric patients to experienced experts. In 1997, the 'Weerklank' (Resonance Foundation) was founded and has since become an international network, called Intervoice, expanding across Europe, Asia and the Americas.

Emancipation means reconsidering AVHs from a non-psychiatric point of view. The Hearing Voices Movement placed psychiatry in a suspicious or even disapproving light. Some evidence has been found to suggest that the main difference between voice hearers with and without a psychiatric disorder is that the former group do not sufficiently recognize or understand the function of their voices (Honig et al., 1998; Romme and Esher 1996), that is, to point towards former traumatic experiences and their possible resolution. AVHs result from life events that the person is unable to solve. Psychiatric symptoms are distinguished and conceived of as secondary reactions to frightening AVHs. The extraordinary experience of AVHs is explained through reasoning as extraordinary as AVHs themselves (e.g. attributing a voice to a deceased person who was psychologically important to the voice hearer).

The psychiatric community often speaks of delusional reasoning as secondary to a psychiatric disorder, with hallucination as the primary symptom. The Empowerment Movement consciously restricts their theory of voices to an understandable process of seeking meaning in an extraordinary experience. Meaning seeking or hermeneutics is the search for the function of each voice and for the underlying problem that the voice is signalling. According to the Empowerment Movement, two questions are important in this search: (1) what *persons* do AVHs represent for the patient, and (2) what *problems* do AVHs represent?

The process of learning how to cope with voices proceeds by three stages: confusion, organization and stabilization (Romme and Esher, 1989). In the confusion stage, voices overwhelm, frighten and confuse the voice hearer, and anxiety and powerlessness dominate. Confrontation and analysis of the relationship between voices and life history are contraindicated at this stage, for anxiety may prevent direct discussion of AVHs. Voices regularly forbid disclosure, with threats of horrible penalties varying from increased noise volume to the death of loved ones. In the organization stage the patient experiences a reduction of anxiety, becomes used to the experience, and searches for ways of coping with AVHs and their consequences. Building a positive relationship with AVHs and accepting ownership are pivotal in this stage. Psychoeducation, reading relevant literature and contacting other voice hearers (self-help groups, Intervoice membership) may promote these processes. Voices become more or less accepted as parts of oneself, and as relevant informants that should be given a role in one's life.

The stabilization stage is characterized by regained control and mastery and making steps towards personal development.

Indications and contraindications for Empowerment

Empowerment is a non-professional movement and Intervoice is an international social media-based organization. Membership of the movement is accessible for all interested in voice hearing. The movement enlists therapists that subscribe their viewpoints. Empowerment does not apply (contra-)indications.

Scientific evidence for the effectiveness of Empowerment

So far, neither effectiveness nor rates of adherence have been studied systematically for Empowerment. The effectiveness of this paradigm is suggested mainly by individual case studies.

Chapter 8

Voice Dialogue

Voice Dialogue was developed in 1993 by American psychologists Hal and Sidra Stone, who were influenced by the works of Jung and William James. The basic assumption underlying Voice Dialogue is that a person's personality is composed of many different sub-personalities which may cooperate or oppose each other. Experiences generate the various constituent personality parts that form a systematic network of primary and repudiated 'outcast' sub-personalities. Primary sub-personalities come to the open depending on their effectiveness in a person's context; outcast sub-personalities work in the dark and may induce inner conflicts. Sub-personalities act as antithetic couples.

Corstens (2013) and Stamboliev (1993) have adapted the Voice Dialogue concept to voice hearing. Their voice-hearing version is closely linked to Empowerment (Corstens *et al.*, 2013; Longdon *et al.*, 2012). Voice Dialogue therapists ask the voice hearer's permission to speak directly with the voices (i.e. the outcast sub-personalities). This is done in a respectful, non-condemning and non-judgemental way. The main purpose of this speaking with voices is to get the hidden sub-personalities into the open, and ask them for information about their origin, function and goals. Voice Dialogue presumes that this will help a person to integrate the outcast sub-personalities into his or her systemic personality network. Although Voice Dialogue resembles 'Gestalt therapy', in contrast to that it is the therapist who speaks with the voice. Patients remain in control of continuation or stopping sessions or ending treatment.

The therapeutic process

After introduction of the method and its focus on the reduction of burden, assessment of the characteristics and interpretations of AVH is started with the help of a voices interview (Romme and Escher, 1999). Hope is actively induced by referring to the positive experiences of other voice hearers, and realistic goals are discussed. Next, the patient's willingness to start an objective and neutral discussion between therapist and voices is assessed. The voice (i.e. the sub-personality) is questioned about his or her name, age, etc. and on time and conditions of first appearance, goals to achieve, caretaker function, and so on. Ideally, a dialogue is initiated on how voice and voice hearer can cooperate to improve the patient's life. Most of time, this discloses hidden emotional vulnerabilities and deficiencies of the patient. Voices may even advise on how the patient can improve quality of life and how to deal with conflicts.

Indications and contraindications for Voice Dialogue

Explicit patient commitment to the method is an absolute requirement. The ability to communicate with one's AVHs is also required.

Contraindications include severe confusion and the initial stage of a first psychotic episode.

Scientific evidence for the effectiveness of Voice Dialogue

So far, neither the effectiveness nor rates of adherence have been studied systematically for Voice Dialogue. It rests on case reports, which suggest most patients to have dissociative and other non-schizophrenic diagnoses (Corstens and Longdon, 2013). So far, no scientific study has been published on the effectiveness of Voice Dialogue.

Part 5

Insight-oriented psychotherapies not specifically aimed at voice hearing

Chapter 9

Psychodynamic psychotherapy

Few RCTs concerning the effectiveness of insight-giving psychotherapies have been done, if at all. In psychodynamic and experiential treatment this is partly due to their frames of reference. Effectiveness studies for both psychodynamic psychotherapy and the experiential or client-centred psychotherapy discussed in Chapter 10 face a tricky problem of protocol because therapies are highly individualized, which interferes with controlled study designs.

Psychodynamic theory considers symptoms (e.g. AVH) as representations of inner conflicts between ego, id and super-ego that have their origin in early childhood. Treatment focuses on this postulated hidden inner conflict. Depending on the psychodynamic school, this conflict may vary from object decathexis (Freud) to ego-boundaries decathexis (Federn, 1952), disturbed mother–child relationship (Mahler, 1952; Sullivan, 1962) and superposition of disturbed object relations on neurobiological constitution (Robbins, 1992). Symptom treatment (e.g. focusing on AVHs) is considered as contraindicated.

The therapeutic process

To facilitate the introspective process therapy sessions are scheduled at the same time and same place, and preferably once to five times a week. Patients are expected to reflect on their experiences, feelings, behaviours and dreams. They are stimulated to freely associate on these in order to enter the deeper underlying conflict. The therapist helps the patient to interpret present behaviours and dreams as repetitions of childhood experiences and interprets here-and-now reactions as harmful defence mechanisms aimed at avoiding the pain of former not yet resolved conflicts.

Indications and contraindications for psychodynamic psychotherapy

Indications are personal suffering and the need for introspection and change. AVH itself is neither an indication nor a target symptom.

Contraindications are severe substance abuse, acting-out inner conflicts, a tendency to externalization, insufficient ability for self-reflection and verbalization.

Scientific evidence for the effectiveness of psychodynamic psychotherapy

Patients' satisfaction with psychodynamic psychotherapy appeared to be less related to their psychiatric state than to the degree of success (Ruocchio, 1989). Culberg and Levander (1991) reported that full recovery is possible; however their claim rested on eight patients only. In schizophrenia patients the effectiveness of additional psychodynamic treatment did not significantly differ from that of other forms of psychotherapy (Mojtabai *et al.*, 1998). However, in controlled studies negative results for psychodynamic psychotherapy prevailed over positive to such an extent that the authors concluded this treatment to be contraindicated in schizophrenia and related disorders (McGlashan, 1994; Mueser and Berenbaum, 1990).

Chapter 10

Experiential or client-centred psychotherapy (ECp)

Experiential or client-centred psychotherapy (ECp) hypothesizes that certain attitudes in therapists constitute the necessary and sufficient conditions for therapeutic effectiveness. It also stresses the self-actualizing quality and inherent tendency of the human organism to develop all of its capacities in ways that serve its maintenance. This quality and tendency are considered the motivational forces in therapy. ECp theory assumes that the same principles of psychotherapy apply to all persons and all disorders. The experiential theory postulates that hallucinations are encoded communicative messages that can be understood, provided they can be deciphered (Teusch, 1990). Prouty hypothesized that hallucinations may be due to disturbed reality testing and the inability to make effective and communicative contacts.

Experiential treatment requires a therapist's empathetic internalized participation that is oriented towards reorganization of the patient's personality. In order to restore the patient's inabilities, therapists may have to act as an external ego, reflecting on the patient's situation, facial expression and posture, and reiterating his or her words.

The therapeutic process

ECp aims at therapeutic growth through absorbing written material, experiencing a single therapy session and participating in intensive groups of various kinds (Kaplan and Sadock, 1989: 1482–1492). Therapists' attitudes are considered crucial for success of therapy; these include the therapist's authenticity or congruence, complete acceptance of or unconditional positive regard for the client, and sensitive and accurately empathetic understanding of the client's feelings and personal meaning.

The stages of the process are: the client's increasing freedom to freely express feelings and personal meanings that have to do with self; the ability to accurately differentiate feelings and perceptions and their objects; dealing with discrepancies and incongruence between what is immediately in experience and the client's concept of self; and the recognition that the structures that have guided the client's life are products of his or her own interpretation, not real external structures.

Indications and contraindications for ECp

Indications are introspective ability, normal intelligence and verbalization ability.

Contraindications are acting-out and externalization. Insufficient ability for self-reflection and verbalization are relative contraindications.

Scientific evidence for the effectiveness of ECp

Clients' satisfaction with ECp appeared to be related to their psychiatric state: the lower their paranoia and confusion, the higher their contentment. Some Belgian centres have published positive case reports of ECp (Deleu and van Werde, 1998; Lietaer *et al.*, 1990). In a pre–post design, stress, frustration, somatic and depressive complaints improved with ECp (Teusch, 1986). Schizophrenic patients treated with ECp improved significantly more in communication than patients in the control condition (Hinterkopf and Brunswick, 1981). However, improvements in psychosocial functioning and psychopathology were similar in both groups (Hinterkopf and Brunswick, 1981; Rogers, 1976). Based on the Wisconsin study data, Truax (1970) concluded that ECp may harm psychotic patients even when provided by experienced therapists.

Chapter 11

Conclusions

Recent developments in psychosocial treatments for AVH are promising. They share a focus on psychological adjustment, engagement and the empowerment of voice hearers despite their differences in implementation and theoretical orientation. In the absence of effectiveness studies, one can only speculate on the effectiveness of some therapies. Some authors doubt the effectiveness of insight-oriented therapies.

As yet, only CBTp and HIT have shown strong evidence-based effects. CBTp is effective on positive psychotic symptoms in general. The individual version has beneficial to modest effects on AVH. The effectiveness beyond the target symptoms is meagre if at all compared to TAU. Some studies report positive effect too on negative psychotic symptoms. Group CBTp certainly improves self-esteem through reduced feelings of social isolation. However, improvements in other areas, AVH included, are equivocal and unimpressive.

Empowerment and Voice Dialogue report interesting results. However, they still await scientific evidence.

Compared with other therapies, HIT has proved effective. Its effects also generalize well beyond the target symptom AVH. The satisfaction of patients is high and drop-out rates are relatively low. Effect sizes and numbers needed to treat AVH are good for HIT compared to CBTp, as are the results on social functioning and quality of life. At present, studies on the natural effectiveness in young, intellectually disabled and autistic patients are in progress. The preliminary results are promising.

Dear reader

If you are interested to know more about HIT, please don't hesitate to contact me. If you want information about a HIT training programme please let me know. The possibilities are formal HIT training (a six day course), 10 days live supervision and consultation.

Jack A. Jenner

J.A.Jenner@hotmail.com

Auditory Vocal Hallucination Rating Scale (AVHRS)

The AVHRS (Jenner and van de Willige, 2002) is a structured interview to obtain detailed information about a patient's auditory vocal hallucinations in the past month. For clinical and/or research purposes it is possible to evaluate one or more other time periods (e.g. past week, past year, lifetime). In the example below, one period is given: past month (mth), plus an opportunity to choose another period.

Rate the highest score that ever occurred in the time period, but if in doubt between two scores select the lowest.

Rate '8' if the answer remains unclear, even after thorough probing.

Rate '9' if the question was not asked.

Mandatory questions **(Mq)** are in **bold**.

Optional questions *(Oq)* are in *italic*.

Name: _____

Gender: M/F

Date of birth: _____

Diagnosis: _____

Date of administration: _____ **Interviewer:** _____

Duration of hearing voices: _____ **months/years**

Hallucinations in other modalities:

    (month)   **visual/olfactory/taste/tactile**

    (. . .)   **visual/olfactory/taste/tactile**

1a. Number of voices

Mq: How many voices did you hear in the past month, was it always just one voice or were there more voices?

Specify number of voices (past month: ..../other period: ....)

Note: If the patient heard only one voice, the next question can be skipped, but tick 1 at question 1b.

Remember to ask about 'the voice' instead of 'the voices' in the following questions.

1b. Separately or simultaneously

In case of multiple voices, ask:

Mq: Are these voices speaking separately (one by one) or together at the same time?

mth		
0	0	No voices in the given time period, or less than once a month
1	1	Always **one** voice
2	2	Several voices, always speaking **separately**; number of voices: . . .
3	3	Several voices, (occasionally) speaking **simultaneously**; number of voices: . . .
8	8	Not clear, even after probing
9	9	Not asked

2. Hypnagogic and/or hypnopompic voices

Mq: At what time of day do you hear the voice(s)?

Note: Ask all item responses.

mth		
1	1	There are only voices when **falling asleep**
2	2	There are only voices during **waking up**
3	3	There are voices **when falling asleep and during waking up**, but not at other times
4	4	The voices may occur **at all times**; when falling asleep, during waking up and at other times

8	8	Not clear, even after probing
9	9	Not asked

3. Frequency

Mq: How often do you hear voices?

Note: If the response is unclear, present all response options.

mth		
0	0	No voices in the given time period, or less than once a month (specify frequency: ....)
1	1	At least **once a week**
2	2	At least **once a day**
3	3	At least **once an hour**
4	4	**Continuously**, or with occasional interruptions of a few minutes*)
8	8	Not clear, even after probing
9	9	Not asked

*Scoring 4 on this question, implies a score of 4 on the next question also. In this case question 4 can be skipped. (Note: tick 4 for 'duration'.)

4. Duration

Mq: When you hear voices, how long do they go on for?

Note: If the response is unclear, present all response options.

mth		
0	0	No voices in the given time period, or less than once a month
1	1	Only a few **seconds**, a transient experience
2	2	A few **minutes**
3	3	At least **one hour**

4	4	**Several hours, consecutively** or **continuously**
8	8	Not clear, even after probing
9	9	Not asked

5. Location

Mq: When you hear voices, where does the sound seem to come from?

Oq: From inside or outside your head?

mth		
0	0	No voices in the given time period, or less than once a month
1	1	Only from **inside** the head
2	2	Both from **inside and outside** the head
3	3	Only from **outside** the head, but **close to the ears**
4	4	Only from **outside** the head, **further away**
8	8	Not clear, even after probing
9	9	Not asked

6. Loudness

Mq: How loud are your voices?

Note: If the response is unclear, present all response options.

mth		
0	0	No voices in the given time period, or less than once a month
1	1	**More quiet** than patient's own voice, e.g. whispering
2	2	About **the same** as patient's own voice
3	3	**Louder** than patient's own voice
4	4	Very loud; **shouting or screaming**

| 8 | 8 | Not clear, even after probing |
| 9 | 9 | Not asked |

7. Origin of the voices

Mq: What do you think causes your voices?

Oq: Are the voices caused by something that is related to yourself (for instance your own thoughts, your own feelings, or by stress or anxiety), or are the voices caused by something outside yourself (other persons, spirits, extraterrestrial beings or something like that?

If the patient refers to *external* cause, then ask:

**Mq: You told me that the voices might be caused by ....
How sure are you about that?**

mth		
0	0	No voices in the given time period, or less than once a month
1	1	Patient thinks that the voices are caused **by internal factors only** (they are associated with him/herself)
2	2	Patient thinks that the voices are caused **by mainly internal factors** ($\geq 50\%$), but there may also be external causes
3	3	Patient thinks that the voices are caused **by mainly external factors** ($> 50\%$), but there may also be internal causes
4	4	Patient thinks that the voices are caused **by external factors only**
8	8	Not clear, even after probing
9	9	Not asked

Note: Scoring of question 7: take the average in reference period.

8. Negative content

Mq: Do your voices say unpleasant, negative or annoying things? Or are they mostly neutral?

Mq: Do your voices also say positive things?

Mq: How often do your voices say negative things and how often do they say positive (or neutral) things?

Oq: Could you give me some examples of what the voices are saying? (Make a note of these examples.)

....

....

....

mth		
0	0	The voices **never** say unpleasant, negative or annoying things
1	1	The voices only **occasionally** say unpleasant, negative or annoying things
2	2	**More than occasionally but less than half** of what the voices say is unpleasant, negative or annoying
3	3	**Half or more** of what the voices say is unpleasant, negative or annoying
4	4	**Every time** the voices say unpleasant, negative or annoying things
8	8	Not clear, even after probing
9	9	Not asked

Note: If it is clear from question 8 that the voices are not unpleasant, negative or annoying, score 0 on question 9, and continue with question 10.

9. Severity of negative content

Mq: You told me that the voices are unpleasant, negative or annoying. Do they say unpleasant, negative or annoying things about you or your family or only about other people? Or do they say only annoying things like cursing?

Mq: Do the voices forbid you to do certain things, like: 'Don't do this or that' or 'Don't tell or say this or that'?

Mq: Do the voices threaten you, or do they say that you have to hurt yourself or other people?

mth		
0	0	The voices are **not unpleasant, negative or annoying**
1	1	The voices are unpleasant, negative or annoying to a certain extent, but **not unpleasant about the patient or his/her family** (e.g. voices cursing or making remarks about other people)
2	2	The voices are saying unpleasant, negative or annoying things about the *behaviour* **of the patient or his/her family**, but not about the patient (e.g. 'You're acting crazy or stupid' or 'Your family doesn't want to see you any more')
3	3	The voices are saying unpleasant, negative or annoying things about **the patient or his/her family** *themselves* (e.g. 'You are ugly, disturbed, mad, . . . ' or 'Your parents are mad . . . ').
4	4	The voices are **threatening** the patient and/or are **giving orders** (e.g. instructions to hurt him/herself or others, to injure or grieve his/herself or his/her family)
8	8	Not clear, even after probing
9	9	Not asked

10. Frequency of distress or suffering

Mq: How often do you suffer from the voices?

Note: If the response is unclear, present all response options.

mth		
0	0	The voices **never** cause distress or suffering
1	1	The voices **sometimes** cause distress or suffering, but less than 50% of the time
2	2	**Half of the time** the voices cause distress or suffering
3	3	**Most of the time** the voices cause distress or suffering

4	4	The voices **always** cause distress or suffering
8	8	Not clear, even after probing
9	9	Not asked

Note: Scoring 0 on question 10, implies a score of 0 on question 11. In this case please tick 0 on the next question.

11. Intensity of distress or suffering

Mq: You just said you suffer from the voice(s). Could you tell me to what extent this affects you? How much do you suffer emotionally from them?

Note: If the response is unclear, present all response options.

mth		
0	0	The voices do **not** cause distress or suffering
1	1	The voices cause **some** distress or suffering
2	2	The voices cause **serious** distress or suffering
3	3	The voices cause **severe** distress or suffering, but it could be worse
4	4	The voices cause **extreme** distress or suffering, the worst that one could imagine
8	8	Not clear, even after probing
9	9	Not asked

12. Interference with daily functioning

Mq: To what extent do the voices interfere with your daily life?

Oq: Do your voices interfere with chores and daily activities like work, study, housekeeping, shopping or other activities?

Oq: Do you get into trouble with your family or friends because of the voices? Can you give me an example?

Oq: Have the voices kept you from proper self-care, like washing or getting properly dressed, etc.

mth		
0	0	**No interference** with daily functioning. Patient is capable of living independently, without problems in daily activities. Patient is able to maintain social and family relationships (if any)
1	1	**Limited interference** with daily functioning. The voices may affect concentration, but everyday activities and social and family relationships can be maintained. Patient can live without additional support
2	2	**Moderate interference** with daily functioning. Some restrictions in everyday activities and/or social and family relationships. Patient is able to live at home, but needs support and/or coaching with everyday activities or supported employment
3	3	**Severe interference** with daily functioning. Patient is frequently on sick leave and/or has job support. Day treatment or outpatient treatment may often be required. Patient keeps some everyday activities, self-care and social relationships
4	4	**Complete interference** with daily functioning. Because of the voices hospitalization is required. Inability to maintain everyday activities and relationships. Self-care is severely disrupted
8	8	Not clear, even after probing
9	9	Not asked

13. Control

Mq: Do you feel that you can manage or control your voices?

Oq: For instance, can you evoke them or let them disappear? Do they listen to you and do they do what you want them to do?

mth		
0	0	Patient has **full control** over the voices; he/she can evoke them and let them disappear whenever he/she wants to
1	1	Patient has **some control** over the voices **most of the time**

2	2	Patient has **some control** over the voices **half of the time**
3	3	Patient has **some control** over the voices **only occasionally**
4	4	Patient has **no control** over the voices; he/she can never evoke them, nor let them disappear
8	8	Not clear, even after probing
9	9	Not asked

14. Anxiety

Mq: Do the voices make you anxious?

Note: If the response is unclear, present all response options.

mth		
0	0	The voices **never cause** anxiety
1	1	The voices **hardly ever** cause anxiety
2	2	The voices **sometimes** cause anxiety
3	3	The voices cause anxiety **most of the time**
4	4	**Sometimes** patient gets **completely into a panic** because of the voices
8	8	Not clear, even after probing
9	9	Not asked

15. Interference

Mq: Do the voices interfere with your thoughts and thinking?

Note: If the response is unclear, present all response options.

mth		
0	0	No, the voices **never** interfere with thinking
1	1	No, the voices **hardly ever** interfere with thinking

2	2	Yes, the voices **sometimes** interfere with thinking
3	3	Yes, **most of the time** the voices interfere with thinking
4	4	Yes, **always** interfere with thinking
8	8	Not clear, even after probing
9	9	Not asked

16. 1st, 2nd or 3rd person voices

Explanation: Voices representing aloud patient's own thoughts are called 1st person voices. Voices talking to the patient or giving him/her instructions are called 2nd person voices. Voices talking with each other about the patient are called 3rd person voices. All three kinds of voices may be present, so rate all that apply.

Mq: Do the voices say aloud what you are thinking? For instance, 'Oh, I am stupid' (if yes, score 1st person)

Mq: Are the voices talking to you? For instance, 'You are stupid' (if yes, score 2nd person)

Mq: Are the voices talking with each other about you? For instance, 'Look, he/she is doing the same stupid things again' (if yes, score 3rd person)

mth		
0	0	No voices in the given time period, or less than once a month
0	0	No voices in the **1st person**
1	1	Yes, there are voices in the **1st person**; number: . . .
8	8	Not clear, even after probing
9	9	Not asked
0	0	No voices in the **2nd person**
1	1	Yes, there are voices in de **2nd person**; number: . . .
8	8	Not clear, even after probing

9	9	Not asked
0	0	No voices in the **3rd person**
1	1	Yes, there are voices in the **3rd person**; number: . . .
8	8	Not clear, even after probing
9	9	Not asked

AVHRS: scoring form

Id patient: ....

Date: ....

Rater: ....

Past month: ....

1a	Number of voices			
1b	Separately or simultaneously			
2	Hypnagogic and/or hypnopompic voices			
3	Frequency			
4	Duration			
5	Location			
6	Loudness			
7	Origin of the voices			
8	Negative content			
9	Severity of negative content			
10	Frequency of distress or suffering			
11	Intensity of distress or suffering			
12	Interference with daily functioning			
13	Control			
14	Anxiety			

15	Interference with thinking			
16	1st, 2nd or 3rd person voices	1st		
		2nd		
		3rd		

Duration of hearing voices: _____ **months/years**

Hallucinations in other modalities:

    (mth)   **visual/olfactory/taste/tactile**

    (...........)   **visual/olfactory/taste/tactile**

Positive and Useful Voices Inventory (PUVI)

The Positive and Useful Voices Inventory (PUVI) is a self-report inventory (Jenner *et al.*, 2008).

Positive voices are the ones that you (the voice hearer) experience as enjoyable, pleasurable or positive.

Useful voices are the ones that you (the voice hearer) experience either positively or negatively, but have a clear useful function.

1   The first voice that you heard was . . . (fill in A and B)

   A   Positive
       As positive as they are negative
       Negative

   B   Useful
       As useful as they are negative
       Not useful

2   The voices that you have heard during the last four weeks have been . . . (fill in A and B)

   A   Positive
       As positive as they are negative
       Negative
       Not applicable

   B   Useful
       As useful as they are negative
       Not useful
       Not applicable

3   Has the *nature* of your voices changed as time has gone by?

   1   Yes, my positive voices have become negative.
   2   Yes, my negative voices have become positive.
   3   Yes, my positive and negative voices have changed their nature.
   4   No, the nature of my voices has stayed the same.

4 Has the *function* of your voices changed as time has gone by?

   1 Yes, my useful voices have lost their utility.
   2 Yes, my non-useful voices have become useful.
   3 No, the function hasn't changed.

5 If changes have happened, what do you think the change depends on?

   1 Personal factors, like for example my capacity of authority, my mood or the image I have of myself.
   2 Exterior factors, such as stress.
   3 Psychiatric treatment that I have received due to my voices.
   4 The changes depend on my voices.
   5 Something else, (please specify)....................
   6 My voices haven't changed in nature or in function.

1st part: positive voices

This is the part of the survey that is about positive voices. These questions refer to positive voices that you have heard in the past month, or if you have stopped hearing them, during the last month that you heard positive voices. If you have never heard voices that you think of as positive, go to question number 23.

6 As time has gone by, the number of positive voices that I have heard has:

   1 Increased
   2 Decreased
   3 Stayed the same

7 What is the average number of times in a period of four weeks that you have heard the highest number of voices?

   1 Continually
   2 Daily, . . . times a day
   3 Weekly, . . . times a week
   4 Monthly, . . . times a month

8 Do the positive voices sound like people you know?

Yes
No
Sometimes they do, sometimes they don't
I don't know

9 Do the positive voices talk to you or about you?

The positive voices talk to me personally (i.e. they tell me 'you have to do this').
The voices talk (individually or between themselves) about me (i.e. 'he/she has to do this').
Voices are directed toward me personally and also talk about me.

10   Have the positive or negative voices ever had control over one another?

Yes, my negative voices have control over my positive voices.
Yes, my positive voices have control over my negative voices.
Yes, my positive and negative voices take turns in controlling one another.
No, my voices do not have control over each other.

11   Do the positive voices help you to cope with the negative ones?

Yes
No
I don't know

Fill out the most correct number in the following 11 questions: 1 (Totally disagree), 2, 3, 4, or 5 (Completely agree)

About my positive voices:	Totally disagree				Completely agree
12 I have them under control	1	2	3	4	5
13 Make me happy	1	2	3	4	5
14 They keep me calm and make me feel better	1	2	3	4	5
15 They make me feel secure about myself	1	2	3	4	5
16 They make me important	1	2	3	4	5
17 They keep me company	1	2	3	4	5
18 They want to protect me	1	2	3	4	5
19 They let me do nice things	1	2	3	4	5
20 They let me have fun (i.e. they make jokes)	1	2	3	4	5
21 They support me	1	2	3	4	5
22 I want to keep them.	1	2	3	4	5

2nd part: useful voices

This part of the test is about useful voices. These questions refer to useful voices that you have heard during the last month, or if you have stopped hearing them, during the last month that you heard the voices. If you have never heard voices that you have thought of as useful, you have finished the test. Thank you for your cooperation.

23   As time has gone by, the number of useful voices that I have heard has:

Increased
Decreased
Stayed the same

24   I feel my useful voices are:

Negative
As negative as they are positive.
Positive

25   What is the average number of times in a period of four weeks that you have heard the highest number of useful voices?

Continually
Daily, . . . times a day

Weekly, . . . times a week
Monthly, . . . times a month

26 Do the useful voices talk to you or about you?

The useful voices talk to me personally (i.e. they tell me 'you have to do this'.
The voices talk (individually or between themselves) about me (i.e. 'he/she
   has to do this').
Voices are directed toward me personally and also talk about me.

27 Do the useful voices help you to cope with the negative ones?

Yes
No
I don't know

Fill out the most correct number in the following 12 questions: 1 (Totally disagree), 2, 3, 4, or 5 (Completely agree)

About my useful voices:	Totally disagree				Completely agree
28 I have them under control	1	2	3	4	5
29 They help me solve problems	1	2	3	4	5
30 They help me keep to my commitments	1	2	3	4	5
31 They help me in my day-to-day life	1	2	3	4	5
32 They help me with financial matters	1	2	3	4	5
33 They help me look after my physical appearance	1	2	3	4	5
34 They help me keep my social contacts	1	2	3	4	5
35 They help me carry out my profession	1	2	3	4	5
36 They help me do my studies	1	2	3	4	5
37 They help me to develop my talent	1	2	3	4	5
38 I want to keep them	1	2	3	4	5
39 They help me maintain my health (physically or mentally).	1	2	3	4	5

Coping with Voices Inventory (CVI)

This is a self-report inventory designed to determine the patient's habitual coping repertoire (Jenner and Geelhoed-Jenner, 1998).

Name: _____

Birth date: _____

File number: _____

Assessment date: _____

Assessor: _____

Therapist: _____

	Applied? (No = 0, Sometimes = 1, Frequently = 2)	Consistent? (No = 0, Yes = 1)	Effective? (No = 0, Little bit = 1, Sufficiently = 2)	Did you stop? And for what reason?
AVH activities:				
Talking (to yourself)				
Talking (with others)				
Telephone				
Praying				
Singing				
Humming				
Reading aloud				
Other				

Motor activities:				
Walking				
Jogging				
Cycling				
Writing				
Other				
Chemical influence:				
Alcohol				
Drugs				
Food				
Starvation				
Drinking (non-alcoholic)				
Bicarbonate of soda				
Medication				
Homeopathic medication				
Other				
Cognitive action I:				
Ignoring				
Evocation in mind				
Self-reassurance				
Thought stop				
Re-attribution				
Other				
Cognitive action II				
Distraction				
Focusing				
Other				

Talking with AVH				
Abusing				
Negotiating				
Asking for advice				
Evocation of AVH				
Conversing				
Other				
Voice-related action				
Performing commands				
Resisting AVHs				
Other				
Physical activities				
Earplugs, etc.				
Listening to music				
Earphones				
Self-punishment (physical)				
Automutilation				
Watching television				
Other				
Social activities				
Withdrawal				
Contacting significant other				
Contacting therapist				
Other				

Physiological action				
Sleeping				
Relaxation				
Other				
Spirituality				
Meditation				
Silent prayer				
Reading religious literature				
Attending religious meeting				
Spiritual rituals				
Other				

Voices Monitoring List

Name:	Day:	Date:			
My voice says	Intensity of suffering (1–10)	Circumstances	Feelings	Thoughts	Actions
		Where are you?			
		Who is present?			

TRAMAL (Trauma List)

TRAMAL is a self-report list on traumatic experiences (Jenner, 2008b).

File number: _____

Name: _____

Birth date: _____

Diagnosis/DSM-IV-TR: _____

Voice hearing ever?:	[ ] yes	[ ] no
Voice hearing past month?:	[ ] yes	[ ] no
Other types of hallucinations?:	[ ] yes	[ ] no

Which ones? _____

Traumatic Experiences List

---

1   Have you been been bullied more than other persons at school or at work?
[ ] never
[ ] once
[ ] sometimes
[ ] regularly
[ ] often
[ ] very often

1a If so, how serious did it feel?	By whom?	And by how many people?
[ ] not at all	[ ] family member	[ ] one person
[ ] a little	[ ] acquaintance	[ ] >one person
[ ] rather	[ ] stranger(s)	
[ ] serious		
[ ] very serious		

2   Have you ever been blackmailed or been completely wrongly punished?
[ ] never
[ ] once

[ ] sometimes
[ ] regularly
[ ] often
[ ] very often

2a If so, how serious did it   By whom?   And by how many
feel?   people?
[ ] not at all   [ ] family member   [ ] one person
[ ] a little   [ ] acquaintance   [ ] >1 person
[ ] rather   [ ] stranger(s)
[ ] serious
[ ] very serious

3 Have you ever experienced physical assault (beating, kicking, etc.)?
[ ] never
[ ] once
[ ] sometimes
[ ] regularly
[ ] often
[ ] very often

3a If so, how serious did it   By whom?   And by how may
feel?   people?
[ ] not at all   [ ] family member   [ ] one person
[ ] a little   [ ] acquaintance   [ ] >1 person
[ ] rather   [ ] stranger(s)
[ ] serious
[ ] very serious

4 Has anyone ever sexually approached or touched you or forced you to
sexual contact or to have intercourse?
[ ] never
[ ] once
[ ] sometimes
[ ] regularly
[ ] often
[ ] very often

4a If so, how serious did it   By whom?   And by how many
feel?   persons?
[ ] not at all   [ ] family member   [ ] one person
[ ] a little   [ ] acquaintance   [ ] >1 person
[ ] rather   [ ] stranger(s)

[ ] serious
[ ] very serious

5   Have you ever seen someone being threatened?
[ ] never
[ ] once
[ ] sometimes
[ ] regularly
[ ] often
[ ] very often

5a If so, how serious did it feel?	By whom?	By how many persons?
[ ] not at all	[ ] family member	[ ] one person
[ ] a little	[ ] acquaintance	[ ] >1 person
[ ] rather	[ ] stranger(s)	
[ ] serious		
[ ] very serious		

6   Have you ever witnessed the murder of someone?
[ ] never
[ ] once
[ ] sometimes
[ ] regularly
[ ] often
[ ] very often

6a If so, how serious did it feel?	By whom?	And by how many persons?
[ ] not at all	[ ] family member	[ ] one person
[ ] a little	[ ] acquaintance	[ ] >1 person
[ ] rather	[ ] stranger(s)	
[ ] serious		
[ ] very serious		

SPITE (Spirituality and Religiosity Test)

This is a self-report test on spirituality and religiosity (Jenner, 2008c).

File number: _____

Name: _____

Birth date: _____

Diagnosis/DSM-IV: _____

Voice hearing ever:	[ ] yes	[ ] no
Voice hearing past month:	[ ] yes	[ ] no
Other types of hallucinations?:	[ ] yes	[ ] no

Which ones? _____

1 Do you believe in God, Allah, Krishna or a supernatural spiritual steering power?
   [ ] Yes, I do in ....
   ....
   [ ] No, Proceed with question 3

2 Do you experience your belief as:
   [ ] supportive, helpful or positive
   [ ] oppressive/negative
   [ ] intermittently positive and negative
   [ ] different, namely

3 Are you religiously or spiritually active at present, for example do you pray, visit sermons or practise rituals?
   [ ] Yes, would you please give examples?
   ....
   ....
   [ ] No

4 Are you a member of a religious group or church at present?
   [ ] Yes, namely
   [ ] No, proceed to question 6

5   Which activities do you do in your religious/ spiritual community?
     [ ] Yes, I perform the following activities
     ....
     ....
     [ ] No, I am not active

6   Have you been religiously raised
     [ ] Yes
     [ ] No, proceed to question 8

7   How did you experience your religious upbringing?
     [ ] Positive
     [ ] Negative
     [ ] Positive as well as negative

8   Have you ever heard 'voices'?
     [ ] Yes, namely . . .
     [ ] No. You may stop filling out this questionnaire

9   Have your 'voices' a religious/spiritual origin?
     [ ] Yes, namely . . .
     [ ] No

10   Have your 'voices' a religious/spiritual content?
     [ ] Yes, please give some examples
     ....
     ....
     [ ] No

11   How do you experience these voices?
     [ ] Positive
     [ ] Negative
     [ ] Both positive and negative

12   Is the function of the 'voices' useful?
     [ ] Yes
     [ ] Intermittently yes and no
     [ ] No

13   Does your belief offer you ways of coping with your voices?
     [ ] Yes, please give some examples
     ....
     ....
     [ ] No

Thanks for filling out this inquiry!

Traffic light crisis prevention plan

This is a crisis and relapse prevention plan (Jenner, 2014).

Structure of the crisis prevention plan:

Alertness for warning signs
Apply AVH coping strategies

Risk factors/situations:

> Which ones?
> How to prevent/avoid these?
> Coping strategies in case of

Assistance

> When?
> Which kind of help?
> By whom?

Special attention

Pivotal in this crisis prevention plan are the search of and insight in feelings, thoughts and behaviour followed by ordering them in three sections according to the colours of traffic lights. Red means you have passed the barrier and are out of control and in crisis, green means you are at rest and stable, while orange is in the middle. Red requires immediate implementation of the crisis plan, pivotal in green is enjoyment and realization of your strength, and orange means start preventive activities. Using the traffic light plan is highly personal and requires dedication and usually necessitates professional help.

Some examples of the traffic light: (1) red = aggressive, angry, chaotic, **severely** depressed, drunk, hopeless, lonely, out of control, restless, signs of depression, suicidal etc.; (2) green = at ease, pleasant, stable, satisfied, at rest; (3) orange = alarming changes in thoughts, feelings and behaviour, automutilation, confusion, irritation, running thoughts, drinking, gambling, hopelessness, etc.

Crisis plan

Warning signs, orange traffic light: ....

....

Coping with AVH:

Three staged coping strategy:

   1 3 minutes ....

   2 5 minutes ....

   3 15 minutes ....

Risk factors/situations:

My risk factors are ....

....

Preventive actions and activities ....

....

Optimal preventive coping strategies...

....

When am I asking for help?

At what time?...

What type of help? ....

From whom?..

References

Aleman A, Larøi F (2008). Hallucinations. *The science of idiosyncratic perception.* Washington, DC: American Psychological Association.

Almeida O, Forst H, Howard R, *et al.* (1993). Unilateral auditory hallucinations. *Br J Psychiatry* 162: 262–264.

Amador S (1994). Teaching medical physics to general audiences. *Biophys J* 66(6): 2217–2221.

Amador XF, Friedman JH, Kasapis C, *et al.* (1996). Suicidal behavior in schizophrenia and its relationship to awareness of illness. *Am J Psychiatry* 153: 1185–1188.

American Psychiatric Association (1994). *Diagnostic and statistical manual of mental disorders* (4th edn). Washington, DC: American Psychiatric Association.

Asaad G, Shapiro B (1986). Hallucinations: theoretical and clinical overview. *J Psychiatry* 143: 1088–1097.

Atkinson JR, Gleeson K, Cromwell J, O'Rourke S (2007). Exploring the perceptual characteristics of voice-hallucinations in deaf people. *Cogn Neuropsychiatry* 12: 339–361.

Bach P, Hayes C (2002). The use of ACT to prevent the rehospitalization of psychotic patients: a RCT. *J Consulting Clin Psychol* 70(5): 1129–1139.

Bak M, Spil van der F, Gunther N, *et al.* (2001). Assessment of Coping Strategies (MACS-I): a brief instrument to assess coping with psychotic symptoms. *Acta Psychiatr Scand* 103: 453–459.

Barrett TR, Etheridge JB (1992). Verbal hallucinations in normals. I: people who hear voices. *Appl Cogn Psychol* 6: 379–387.

Bartels-Velthuis AA, Jenner JA, Willige van de G, *et al.* (2010). Prevalence and correlates of auditory vocal hallucinations in middle childhood. *Br J Psychiatry* 196: 41–46.

Bartels-Velthuis AA, Willige van de G, Jenner JA, *et al.* (2011). Course of auditory vocal hallucinations in childhood: 5-year follow-up study. *Br J Psychiatry* 199: 296–302.

Bartels-Velthuis AA, Willige van de G, Jenner JA, *et al.* (2012a). Consistency and reliability of the Auditory Vocal Hallucination Rating Scale (AVHRS). *Epidemiol Psychiatr Sci* 21(3): 305–310.

Bartels-Velthuis AA, Willige van de G, Jenner JA, *et al.* (2012b). Auditory hallucinations in childhood: associations with adversity and delusional ideation. *Psychol Med* 42(3): 583–593.

Benjamin LS (1989). Is chronicity a function of the relationship between the person and the auditory hallucination? *Schizophr Bull* 15: 291–310.

Bennett BM (1978). Vision and audition in biblical prophecy. *Parapsychol Rev* 9: 1–12.

Bentall RP, Haddock G, Slade PD (1994). Cognitive behaviour therapy for persistent auditory hallucinations: from theory to therapy. *Behav Ther* 25: 51–66.

Bentall RP, Wickham S, Shevlin M, Varese F (2012). Do specific early-life adversities lead to specific symptoms of psychosis? A study from the 2007 Adult Psychiatric Morbidity Survey. *Schizophr Bull* 38(4): 734–740.

Berrios G (1990). Musical hallucinations: a historical and clinical study. *Br J Psychiatry* 156: 188–194.

Birchwood M, Meaden A, Trower, *et al.* (2002). Shame, humiliation, and entrapment in psychosis: a social rank theory approach to cognitive intervention with voices and delusions. In: Morrison AP (ed.) *Casebook of cognitive therapy for psychosis.* London: Brunner-Routledge, pp. 108–131.

Birchwood M, Gilbert P, Gilbert J, *et al.* (2004). Interpersonal and role-related schema influence the relationship with the dominant 'voice' in schizophrenia: a comparison of three models. *Psychol Med* 34(8): 1571–1580.

Byrne P (2003). Adolescent psychiatry in clinical practice. *Child and Adolesc Ment Health* 8(3):151.

Cannon M, Caspi A, Moffit TE, *et al.* (2002). Evidence for early-childhood, pan-developmental impairment specific to schizophreniform disorder. *Arch Gen Psychiatry* 59: 449–456.

Carter DM, MacKinnon A, Copolov DL (1996). Patients' strategies for coping with auditory hallucinations. *J Nerv Ment Dis* 184: 159–164.

Chadwick P, Birchwood M (1994). The omnipotence of voices: a cognitive approach to auditory hallucinations. *Br J Psychiatry* 164(2): 190–201.

Chadwick P, Birchwood M (1996). Cognitive therapy for voices. In: Haddock G, Slade PD (eds) *Cognitive behavioural interventions with psychotic disorders.* London: Routledge.

Chadwick P, Lees S, Birchwood M (2000a). BAVQ-R. *Br J Psychiatry* 177: 229–233.

Chadwick P, Sambrooke S, Rasch S, *et al.* (2000b). Challenging the omnipotence of voices: group-cognitive behavior therapy for voices. *Behav Res Ther* 38(10): 993–1993.

Cheung P, Schweitzer I, Crowley K, *et al.* (1997). Violence in schizophrenia: role of hallucinations and delusions. *Schizophr Res* 26: 181–190.

Clarke MC, Haely M, Cannon M (2006). The role of obstetric events in schizophrenia. *Schizophr Bull* 32: 2–8.

Cohen CI, Berk LA (1985). Personal coping styles of schizophrenic outpatients. *Hosp Community Psychiatry* 36: 407–410.

Cohn-Sherbok D, Cohn-Sherbok L (1997). *Jewish and Christian mysticism: an introduction.* New York: Continuum.

Copolov DL, Mackinnon A, Trauer T (2004). Correlates of the affective impact of auditory hallucinations in psychotic disorders. *Schizophr Bull* 30(1): 163–171.

Cormac I, Jones C, Campbell C (2002). Cognitive behaviour therapy for schizophrenia. *Cochrane Database Syst Rev* (1): CD000524.

Corrigan PW, Lieberman RP, Engel JD (1990). From noncompliance to collaboration in the treatment of schizophrenia. *Hosp Community Psychiatry* 41: 1203–1211.

Corstens D, Longdon E (2013). The origins of voices: links between life history and voice hearing in a survey of 100 cases. *Psychosis* (in press). doi: 10.1080/17522439. 2013.816337

Corstens D, Longdon E, Rydinger B, Bentall R, Os van J (2013). Treatment of hallucinations: a comment. *Psychosis* 5(1): 98–102.

Cramer JA (1991). Overview of methods to measure and enhance patient compliance. In: Cramer JA, Spilker B (eds) *Patient compliance in medical practice and clinical trials.* New York: Raven Press.

Culberg J, Levander S (1991). Fully recovered schizophrenic patients who received intensive psychotherapy: a Swedish case-findings study. *Nord Psykiatr Tidsskr* 45(4): 253–262.

David AS (1999). Auditory hallucinations: phenomenology, neuropsychology and neuro-imaging update. *Acta Psychiatr Scand* 395 (Suppl): 95–104.

Deleu CH, Werde van D (1998). The relevance of a phenomenological attitude when working with psychotic people. In: *Person-centered therapy*. London: Sage, pp. 206–215.

Dickerson FB (2000). Cognitive behavioural psychotherapy for schizophrenia: a review of recent empirical studies. *Schizophr Res* 43: 71–90.

Dixon LB, Lehman AF (1995). Family interventions for schizophrenia. *Schizophr Bull* 21(4): 631–643.

Dyck DG, Short RA, Hendryx MS, *et al.* (2000). Management of negative symptoms among patients with schizophrenia attending multi-family groups. *Psychiatr Serv* 51(4): 513–519.

Eaton WW, Romanovski A, Anthony JC, *et al.* (1991). Screening for psychosis in the general population with a self-report interview. *J Nerv Ment Dis* 179: 689–693.

Escher A (2004). *An exploration of AVH in children and adolescents*. PhD thesis, University of Central England. Birmingham, UK.

Escher S, Romme M, Buiks A, Delespaul P, Os Van J (2002). Independent course of childhood auditory hallucinations: a sequential 3-year follow-up study. *Br J Psychiatry* 43 (Suppl): s10–18.

Esquirol JED (1832). Sur les illusions des sens chez les aliénes. *Archiv Général Méd* 2: 5–23.

Fawcett J (1999). Compliance: definition and key issues. *J Clin Psychiatry* (suppl) 56: 4–8.

Federn P (1952). *Ego psychology and the psychosis*. New York: Basic Books.

Ferreira R (1959). Psychotherapy with severely regressed schizophrenics. *Psychiatr Q* 33: 663–682.

Fisher HL, Caspi A, Poulton R, *et al.* (2013). Specificity of childhood psychotic symptoms for predicting schizophrenia by 38 years of age: a birth cohort study. *Psychol Med* 10: 1–10.

Frith CD (1992). *The cognitive neuropsychology of schizophrenia*. Hove, UK: Lawrence Erlbaum.

Gaag van der M (2012). Cognitive behaviour therapy. In: Jenner JA (ed.) *Hallucinations: characteristics, causal models and treatment* (in Dutch). Assen: VanGorcum, pp. 99–109.

Garety PA, Kuipers E, Fowler D, *et al.* (2001). A cognitive model of the positive symptoms of psychosis. *Psychol Med* 31(2): 189–195.

Garfield SR (1994). The delivery of medical care. *MD Comput* 11(1): 43–47.

Geelhoed-Jenner B, Jenner JA, Wiersma D (2001). Does coping training influence strategies of coping with persistent auditory hallucinations in patients with schizophrenia? *Schizophr Res* 49(1–2, Suppl): 260.

Glaser JP, Os Van J, Thewissen V, *et al.* (2010). Psychotic reactivity in borderline personality disorder. *Acta Psychiatr Scand* 121(2): 125–134.

Goldstone E, Farhall J, Ong B (2012). Modelling the emergence of hallucinations: early acquired vulnerabilities, proximal life stressors and maladaptive psychological processes. *Soc Psychiatry Psychiatr Epidemiol* 47(9): 1367–1380.

Gould RA, Mueser KT, Bolton E, *et al.* (2001). Cognitive therapy for psychosis in schizophrenia: an effect analysis. *Schizophr Res* 48: 335–342.

Grimby A (1993). Bereavement among elderly people: grief reactions, post-bereavement hallucinations and quality of life. *Acta Psychiatr Scand* 87: 72–80.

Haddock G, Bentall RP, Slade PD (1995). Auditory hallucinations and the verbal transformation effect: the role of suggestions. *Person Individ Differ* 19: 301–306.

Haddock G, McCarron J, Tarrier N, *et al.* (1999). Scales to measure dimensions of hallucinations and delusions: the Psychotic Symptom Rating Scale (PSYRATS). *Psychol Med* 29: 879–889.

Hammersley P, Dias A, Todd G, *et al.* (2003). Childhood trauma and hallucinations in bipolar affective disorder: preliminary investigation. *Br J Psychiatry* 182: 543–547.

Haro JM, Arbabzadeh-Bouchez S, Brugha TS, *et al.* (2006). Concordance of the Composite International Diagnostic Interview Version 3.0 (CIDI 3.0) with standardized clinical assessments in the WHO World Mental Health surveys. *Int J Methods Psychiatr Res* 15: 167–180.

Hawton K, Zahl D, Weatherall R, *et al.* (2003). Suicide following deliberate self-harm: long-term follow-up of patients who presented to a general hospital. *Br J Psychiatry* 182: 537–542.

Haynes RB (1976). A critical review of the determinants of patient compliance with therapeutic regimes. In: Sackett DL, Haynes RB (eds) *Compliance with therapeutic regimes.* Baltimore, MD: Johns Hopkins University Press.

Heinssen RK, Liberman RP, Kopelowicz A (2000). Psychosocial skills training for schizophrenia: Lessons from the laboratory. *Schizophr Bull* 26(1): 21–46.

Hepworth CR, Ashcroft K, Kingdon D (2013). Auditory hallucinations: a comparison of beliefs about voices in individuals with schizophrenia and borderline personality disorder. *Clin Psychol Psychother* 20(3): 239–245.

Hinterkopf E, Brunswick L (1981). Teaching mental patients to use client-centered and experiential skills with each other. *Psychother Theory Res Pract* 18(3): 394–402.

Hoffman RE, Hawkins KA, Gueorguieva R, *et al.* (2003). Transcranial magnetic stimulation of left temporoparietal cortex and medication-resistant auditory hallucinations. *Arch Gen Psychiatry* 60: 49–56.

Hogarty GE, Anderson CM, Douglas J, *et al.* (1991). Family psychoeducation, social skills, training, and maintenance chemotherapy in the aftercare treatment of schizophrenia II. Two-year effects of a controlled study on relapse and adjustment. *Arch Gen Psychiatry* 48(4): 340–347.

Holmes EP, Corrigan PW, Williams P, *et al.* (1999). Changing attitudes about schizophrenia. *Schizophr Bull* 25(3): 447–456.

Honig A, Romme MA, Ensink BJ, *et al.* (1998). Auditory hallucinations: a comparison between patients and nonpatients. *J Nerv Ment Dis* 86(10): 646–651.

Inouye J, Shimizu A (1970). The electromyographic study of verbal hallucination. *J Nerv Ment Dis* 151: 415–422.

Jaffe SL (1966). Hallucinations in children in a state hospital. *Psychiatr Q* 2: 88–95.

Janzing C (1966). Steunende groepstherapie voor de chronische patiënt. (Supportive group therapy for chronic patients). Handbook group psychotherapy.

Jaynes J (1979). *The origin of consciousness in the breakdown of the bicameral mind.* Harmondsworth, UK: Penguin.

Jenner JA (1984). *Admission preventive strategies* (in Dutch). PhD thesis, Erasmus University.

Jenner JA (2002). HIT: an integrative treatment for patients with persistent auditory hallucinations. *Psychiatric Services* 53(7): 897–898.

Jenner JA (2008a). Assertive community treatment in the Netherlands. Letter to the editor. *Acta Psychiatr Scand* 117(1): 76–78.

Jenner JA (2008b). *TRAMAL* (Trauma list). Haren, the Netherlands: Jenner Consultants.

Jenner JA (2008c). *SPITE* (Spirituality test). Haren, the Netherlands: Jenner Consultants.

Jenner JA (2010). ACT in het perspectief van EBM. *Mgv* 65(9): 710–718.

Jenner JA (2012a). Beyond monotherapy. In: Jardri R, Thomas P, Pins D (eds) *The neuroscience of hallucinations*. New York: Springer Verlag, pp. 447–471.

Jenner JA (2012b). *Hallucinaties: kenmerken, verklaringen en behandeling* (2nd edn, in Dutch). Assen: VanGorcum.

Jenner JA (2013). *Directieve interventies in de psychiatrie*. Assen: VanGorcum.

Jenner JA (2014). *Traffic light crisis prevention plan*. Haren, the Netherlands: Jenner Consultants.

Jenner JA, Geelhoed-Jenner B (1998). *The Coping with Voices Inventory*. Internal publication UCP, UMCG, Groningen.

Jenner JA, Niesing J (2000). The semantic differential regarding suicide. *Acta Psychiatr Scand* 101: 1–8.

Jenner JA, Tromp C (1998). Modellen van zorg. In: Jenner JA *et al.* (eds) *Wel bezorgd, geestelijke verzorging en gezondheidszorg*. Utrecht: Kok-Kampen.

Jenner JA, Willige van de G (2001). HIT, Hallucination focused Integrative Treatment as early intervention in psychotic adolescents with auditory hallucinations: a pilot study. *Acta Psychiatr Scand* 103: 148–152.

Jenner JA, Willige van de G (2002). *Auditory Vocal Hallucinating Rating Scale (AVHRS)*. Internal publication. UCP, UMCG, Groningen.

Jenner JA, Willige van de G, Wiersma D (1998). Effectiveness of cognitive therapy with coping training for persistent auditory hallucinations: a retrospective study of attenders of a psychiatric outpatient department. *Acta Psychiatr Scand* 98(5): 384–389.

Jenner JA, Mulder H, de Boer R (2001). *HIT-MFT: patient course book & trainer manual* (in Dutch). Groningen: UCP, UMCG.

Jenner JA, Nienhuis FJ, Wiersma D, *et al.* (2004). Hallucination focused Integrative Treatment improves burden, control, and symptoms in schizophrenia patients with drug-resistant hallucinations. *Schizophr Bull* 30: 127–139.

Jenner JA, Willige van de G, Wiersma D (2006a). Multi-family treatment for patients with persistent auditory hallucinations and their relatives. *Acta Psychiatr Scand* 113: 154–158.

Jenner JA, Nienhuis FJ, Willige van de G, Wiersma D (2006b). 'Hitting' voices of schizophrenia patients may lastingly reduce persistent auditory hallucinations and their burden: 18-mth outcome of a randomised controlled trial. *Can J Psychiatry* 51: 169–177.

Jenner JA, Rutten S, Beuckens J, Boonstra N, Sytema S (2008). Positive and useful auditory hallucinations: prevalence, characteristics, attributions, and implications for treatment. *Acta Psychiatr Scand* 118: 238–245.

Jenner JA, Kollen B, Burger H (submitted). Relationship between traumatic experience and AVH.

Johnson CH, Gilmore JD, Shenoy RS (1983). Thought-stopping and anger induction in the treatement of hallucinations and obsessional ruminations. *Psychotherapy Theory Res Pract* 20(4): 445–448.

Johnstone EC, Frith CD, Crow TJ, *et al.* (1991). The Northwick Park 'functional' psychosis study: diagnosis and outcome. *Psychol Med* 22: 331–346.

Kandel D, Raveis V, Davies M (1991). Suicidal ideation in adolescence: depression, substance use, and other risk factors. *J Youth Adolesc* 20: 289–309.

Kaplan HI, Sadock BJ (eds) (1989). *Kaplan and Sadock's comprehensive textbook of psychiatry* (5th edn). Baltimore, MD: Williams & Wilkins, pp. 1482–1492.

Kelleher J, Lynch F, Harley M, *et al.* (2012). Psychotic symptoms in adolescence index for suicidal behaviour: findings from 2 population-based case-control studies. *Arch Gen Psychiatry* 69(12): 1277–1283.

Kelleher I, Corcoran P, Keely H, *et al.* (2013). Psychotic symptoms and populations risk for suicide attempt: implications for suicidality, multimorbidity and functioning. *YAMA Psychiatry* 70(9): 940–948.

Kelleher I, Cederlöf M, Lichtenstein P (2014). Psychotic experiences as a predictor of the natural cause of suicidal ideation: a Swedish cohort study. *World Psychiatry* 13(2): 184–188.

Kienhorst CWM, Dewilde EJ, Vandenbout J, *et al.* (1993). Two subtypes of adolescent suicide attempters: an empirical classification. *Acta Psychiatr Scand* 87: 18–22.

Kuipers E, Fowler D, Garety P, *et al.* (1997). London-East-Anglia RCT of CBT for psychosis. I: effects of the treatment phase. *Br J Psychiatry* 171: 319–327.

Landmark J, Merskey H, Cernovsky ZZ, *et al.* (1990). The positive triad of schizophrenic symptoms: its statistical properties and its relationship to 13 traditional diagnostic systems. *Br J Psychiatry* 156: 388–394.

Lange A (1985). *Gedragsverandering in gezinnen* (5th edn). Groningen: Wolters-Noordhoff.

Lataster T, Os van J, Drukker M, *et al.* (2006). Childhood victimization and developmental expression of non-clinical delusional ideation and hallucinatory experiences. *Soc Psychiatry Psychiatr Epidemiol* 41: 423–425.

Hui-Lin Li (1974). An archaeological and historic account of cannabis in China. *Econom Bot* 28: 437–448.

Liberman RP, CJ Wallace, G Blackwell, *et al.* (1998). Skills training versus psychosocial occupational therapy for persons with persistent schizophrenia. *Am J Psychiatry* 155(8): 1087–1091.

Lietaer G, Rombouts J, Balen van R (eds) (1990). *Client-centered and experiential psychotherapy in the nineties.* Leuven: Leuven University Press.

Lippman TW (1982). *Understanding Islam: an introduction to the Muslim world.* New York: Mentor.

Lobban F, Barrowclough C, Jones C (2004). The impact of beliefs about mental health problems and coping on outcome in schizophrenia. *Psychol Med* 34(7): 1165–1176.

Longdon E, Corstens D, Escher S, *et al.* (2012). Hearing voices in biographical context: a framework to give meaning to voice hearing experiences. *Psychosis* 4(3): 224–234.

Luteijn B, Jenner JA (2012). *Hoe scoren CBT en HIT in gerandomiseerd, gecontroleerd onderzoek?* Poster Conference Dutch Psychiatric Association. Maastricht.

Mackie CJ, Catellanos-Ryan N, Conrod PJ (2011). Developmental trajections of psychotic-like experiences across adolescents. *Psychol Med* 41: 47–58.

Mahler M (1952). On child psychosis and schizophrenia: autistic and symbiotec infantile psychosis. *Psychoanal Study Child* 7: 286–305.

Marder SR (1999). Antipsychotic drugs and relapse prevention. *Schizophr Res* 35: 87–92.

McFarlane WR, Link B, Dushay R, *et al.* (1995a). Psychoeducational multiple family groups: four-year relapse outcome in schizophrenia. *Fam Process* 34: 127–144.

McFarlane WR, Lukens E, Dushay R, *et al.* (1995b). Multiple family group and psychoeducation in the treatment of schizophrenia. *Arch Gen Psychiatry* 52: 679–687.

McGee R, Williams S, Poulton R (2000). Hallucinations in nonpsychotic children. *Acad Adolesc Psychiatry* 39(1): 12–13.

McGlashan TH (1994). What has become of the psychotherapy of schizophrenia? *Acta Psychiatr Scand* 384/5 (Suppl): 147–152.

McKeith IG, Dickson DW, Lowe J, *et al.* (2005). Diagnosis and management of dementia with Lewy bodies: third report of the DIB consortium. *Neurology* 65: 1863–1872.

Miller WR, Rolnick S (1991). *Motivational interviewing: preparing people to change addictive behavior*. New York: Guilford Press.

Mojtabai R, Nicholson RA, Carpenter BN (1998). Role of psychosocial treatments in the management of schizophrenia: a meta-analytic review of controlled outcome studies. *Schizophr Bull* 24(4): 69–87.

Mueser KT, Berenbaum H (1990). Psychodynamic treatment of schizophrenia: is there a future? *Psychol Med* 20: 253–262.

Mueser KT, Bellack AS, Berady EU (1989). Hallucinations in schizophrenia. *Acta Psychiatr Scand* 82: 26–29.

Myin-Germeys I, Delespaul P, Os van J (2005). Behavioural sensitization to daily life stress in psychosis. *Psychol Med* 35(5): 733–741.

Nayani TH, David AS (1996). The auditory hallucination: a phenomological survey. *Psychol Med* 26: 177–189.

Newton E, Landau S, Smith P, *et al.* (2005). Early psychological intervention for auditory hallucinations: an exploratory study of young people's voices groups. *J Nerv Ment Dis* 193: 58–61.

NICE (National Institute for Clinical Excellence) (2011). *Schizophrenia: core interventions in the treatment and management of schizophrenia in primary and seconday care*. London: National Collaborating Centre for Mental Health commissioned by NICE, pp. 117–138.

Nienhuis FJ (2011). *Mini-SCAN*. Groningen: UMCG.

Os van J, Hanssen M, Bijl RV, *et al.* (2000). Strauss (1969) revisited: a psychosis continuum in the general population? *Schizophr Res* 45(1): 11–20.

Os van J, Krabbendam L, Myin-Germeijs I, *et al.* (2005). The schizophrenia envirome. *Curr Opin Psychiatry* 58: 141–145.

Os van J, Linscott RJ, Muin-Germeys I, *et al.* (2009). A systematic review and meta-analysis of the psychosis continuum: evidence for a psychosis proneness-persistence-impairment model of psychotic disorder. *Psychol Med* 39: 179–195.

Os van TWDP, Brink van den RHS, Tiemens BG, *et al.* (2005). Communicative skills of general practitioners augment the effectiveness of guideline-based depression treatment. *J Affect Disord* 84: 43–51.

Penfield W, Kristiansen K (1951). In: *Epileptic seizure patterns*. Springfield, IL: Charles C Thomas, pp. 22–23.

Penn DL, Kommana S, Mansfield M, *et al.* (1999). Dispelling the stigma of schizophrenia: II. the impact of information on dangerousness. *Schizophr Bull* 25(3): 437–446.

Penn DL, Meyer P, Evans E, *et al.* (2009). A randomized controlled trial of group Cognitive-Behavioral Therapy versus Enhanced Supportive Therapy for auditory hallucinations. *Schizophr Res* 109: 52–59.

Pennings MHA, Romme MAJ (1997). *Gespreksgroepen voor mensen die stemmen horen*. Maastricht: University of Maastricht.

Perkins DO (2002). Noncompliance in patients with schizophrenia. *J Clin Psychiatry* 63(12): 1121–1127.

Pilling S, Bebbington P, Kuipers E, *et al.* (2002). Psychological treatment in schizophrenia: I. meta-analysis of family interventions and cognitive behaviour therapy. *Psychol Med* 32: 763–782.

Pitschel-Walz G, Leucht S, Bäuml J, *et al.* (2001). The effect of family interventions on relapse and rehospitalization in schizophrenia: a meta-analysis. *Schizophr Bull* 27(1): 73–92.

Prochaska JO, DiClemente CC (1982). Transtheoretical therapy: towards a more integrative model of change. *Psychotherapy Theory Res Pract* 19: 276–288.

Prochaska JO, DiClemente CC, Norcross JC (1992). In search of how people change: applications to addictive behaviors. *Am Psychol* 47(9): 1102–1114.

Rajerethinam RP, DeQuardo JR, Nalepa R, *et al.* (2000). Superior temporal gyrus in schizophrenia: a volumetric magnetic resonance imaging study. *Schizophr Res* 41: 302–312.

Read J, Perry B, Moskowitz A, *et al.* (2001). The contribution of early traumatic events to schizophrenia in some patients: a traumatogenic neurodevelopmental model. *Psychiatry Interpersonal Biol Processes* 64: 319–345.

Riskind JH, Beck AT, Berchick RJ, *et al.* (1987). Reliability of DSM-III diagnoses for major depression and generalized anxiety disorder using the structured clinical interview for DSM–III. *Arch Gen Psychiatry* 44: 817–820.

Robbins M (1992). Psychoanalytic and biological approaches to mental illness: schizophrenia. *J Am Psychoanal Assoc* 40: 425–454.

Rogers CR (1976). The findings in brief. In: Rogers CR (ed.) *The therapeutic relationship and its impact: a study of psychotherapy with schizophrenics.* Madison, WI: University of Wisconsin Press, pp. 73–93.

Romme MAJ, Escher ADMAC (1989). Hearing voices. *Schizophr Bull* 5(2): 209–216.

Romme MAJ, Escher ADMAC (1999). *Accepting voices.* London: Mind Publications.

Romme M, Escher S (2012). Empowerment and making sense. In: Jenner JA (ed.) *Hallucinaties* (in Dutch). Assen: VanGorcum, pp. 112–122.

Romme MAJ, Honig A, Noorthoorn EO, Escher AD (1992). Coping with voices an emancipatory approach. *Br J Psychiatry* 161: 99–103.

Rössler W, Riecher-Wössler, Angst J, *et al.* (2007). Psychotic experiences in the general population: a twenty-year prospective community study. *Schizophr Res* 92: 1–14.

Roy A (2004). Relationship of childhood trauma to age of first suicide attempt and number of attempts in substance dependent patients. *Acta Psychiatr Scand* 109: 121–125.

Ruocchio PJ (1989). How psychotherapy can help the schizophrenic patient. *Hosp Community Psychiatry* 40: 188–190.

Rutten S, Beuckens J, Boonstra N, *et al.* (2007). Positieve en nuttige auditieve vocale hallucinaties. *Tijdschrift Psychiatrie* 49(11): 803–813.

Sanjuan J, Gonzalez JC, Aquilar EJ, *et al.* (2004). Pleasurable auditory hallucinations. *Acta Psychiatr Scand* 110: 273–278.

Sarbin TR, Juhasz JB (1967). The historical background of the concept of hallucination. *J Hist Behav Sci* 5: 339–358.

Sayer J, Ritter S, Gournay K (2000). Beliefs about voices and their effect on coping strategies. *J Adv Nurs* 31(5): 1199–1205.

Schonauer K, Achtergarde D, Gotthardt U, *et al.* (1998). Hallucinatory modalities in prelingualy deaf schizophrenic patients: a retrospective analysis of 67 cases. *Acta Psychiatr Scand* 89: 377–383.

Shea CC (1998). *Psychiatric interviewing.* Philadelphia, PA: Saunders.

Shevlin M, Hiuston JE, Dorahy MJ, Adamson G (2008). Cumulative traumas and psychosis: an analysis of the national comorbidity survey and the British Psychiatric Morbidity Survey. *Schizophr Bull* 34: 193–199.

Shevlin M, Murphy J, Read J, *et al.* (2011). Childhood adversity and hallucinations: a community-based study using the National Comorbidity Survey Replication. *Soc Psychiatry Psychiatr Epidemiol* 46(12): 1203–1210.

Sidgewick H, Johnson A, Myers FWH, *et al.* (1894). Report on the census of hallucinations. *Proc Soc Psychical Res* 10: 259–393.

Siegler M, Osmond H (1966). Models of madness. *Br J Psychiatry* 112: 1193–1203.

Slade PD, Bentall RP (1988). *Sensory deception: a scientific analysis of hallucination.* London: Croom-Helm.

Slotema CW, Kingdon DG (2012). Auditory vocal hallucinations in patients with borderline personality disorder. *Hallucination* 125–132.

Spauwen J, Krabbendam L, Lieb R, *et al.* (2006). Impact of psychological trauma on the development of psychotic symptoms. *Br J Psychiatry* 188: 527–533.

Stamboliev R (1993). *The energetics of voice dialogue* (in Dutch). Baarn: Mesa Verde.

Stant AD, TenVergert EM, Groen H, *et al.* (2003). Cost-effectiveness of the HIT-programme in patients with schizophrenia and persistent AVH. *Acta Psychiatr Scand* 107: 361–368.

Stephane M, Barton S, Boutros NN (2001). Auditory verbal hallucinations and dysfunction of the neuralsubstrates of speech. *Schizophr Res* 50: 61–78.

Stephane M, Thuras P, Narallah H, *et al.* (2003). The internal structure of the phenomenology of auditory verbal hallucinations. *Schizophr Res* 61: 185–193.

Steuljens B (2012). Groepstherapie. In: *Hallucinaties.* Assen: VanGorcum, pp.134–142.

Sullivan HS (1962). *Schizophrenia as a human process.* New York: Norton.

Tarrier N, Lewis S, Haddock G, *et al.* (2004). Cognitive-behavioural therapy in first-episode and early schizophrenia 18-month follow-up of a randomised controlled trial. *Br J Psychiatry* 184(3): 231–239.

Teusch L (1986). Presprachpsychotherapie schizophrener Patienten. *Zeitschr Oersonenzentrierte Psychol Psychother* 5: 391–398.

Teusch L (1990). Positive effects and limitations of client-centered therapy with schizophrenic patients. In: Lietaer G *et al.* (eds) *Client-centered and experiential psychotherapy in the nineties.* Leuven: Leuven University Press, pp.637–644.

Thomas N, Hayward M, Peters E, *et al.* (2014). Psychological therapies for auditory hallucinations (voices): current status and key directions for future research. *Schizophr Bull* 40(4): 202–212.

Tien AY (1991). Distributions of hallucinations in the population. *Social Psychiatry Psychiatr Epidemiol* 26: 287–292.

Trauer T, Sacks T (2000). The relationship between insight and medication adherence in severely mentally ill clients treated in the community. *Acta Psychiatr Scand* 102: 211–216.

Trower P, Birchwood M, Meaden A, *et al.* (2004). Cognitive therapy for command hallucinations: RCT. *Br J Psychiatry* 184: 312–320.

Truax CB (1970). Effects of client-centered psychotherapy with schizophrenic patients: nine years pre-therapy and nine years post-therapy hospitalization. *J Consult Clin Psychol* 3: 417–422.

Valmaggia LR, Gaag van der M, Tarrier N, *et al.* (2005). CBT for refractory psychotic symptoms of schizophrenia resistant to atypical antipsychotic medication: RCT. *Br J Psychiatry* 186: 324–330.

VandenBos GR (ed.) (2007). *APA dictionary of psychology*. Washington, DC: American Psychological Association.

Verdoux H, Maurice-Tison S, Gay B, *et al.* (1998). A survey of delusional ideation in primary-care patients. *Psychol Med* 28: 127–134.

Walker EF, DiFerio D (1997). A neural diathesis-stress model. *Psychol Res* 21(8): 1143–1192.

Watzlawick P, Beavin JH, Jackson DD (1967). *Pragmatics of human communication: a study of interactional pattern pathologies, and paradoxes*. New York: Norton.

Weiss AP, Heckers S. Thanvi, *et al.* (1999). Neuroimaging of hallucinations: a review of birth cohort studies. *Psychiatry Res* 92: 61–74.

Welham J, Isohanni M, Jones P, *et al.* (2009). The antecedents of schizophrenia: a review of birth cohort studies. *Schizophr Bull* 35: 603–623.

West LJ (1975). A clinical and theoretical overview of hallucinatory phenomena. In: Siegel RK, West LJ (eds) *Hallucinations: behaviour, experience and theory*. New York: John Wiley & Sons.

White M (1986). Negative explanation, restraint and double description: a template for family therapy. *Fam Process* 25(2): 169–184.

Wiersma D, de Jong A, Kraaijkamp HJM, Ormel J (1990). *GSB-II. The Groningen Social Disabilities Schedule. Version 2*. Groningen, Netherlands: Department of Psychiatry, Rijksuniversiteit Groningen.

Wiersma D, Jenner JA, Willige van de G, *et al.* (2001). Cognitive behaviour therapy with coping training for persistent auditory hallucinations in schizophrenia: a naturalistic follow-up study of the durability of effects. *Acta Psychiatr Scand* 103: 393–399.

Wiersma D, Jenner JA, Nienhuis FJ, *et al.* (2004). HIT improves quality of life in schizophrenia patients. *Acta Psychiatr Scand* 109: 194–201.

Woodruff PWR (2004). Auditory hallucinations: insights and questions from neuroimaging. *Cogn Neuropsychiatry* 9(1/2): 73–91.

Wolpe J (1958). *Psychotherapy by reciprocal inhibition*. Stanford: Stanford University Press.

Wunderink L, Nieboer RM, Wiersma D, *et al.* (2013). Recovery in remitted first-episode psychosis at 7 years of follow-up of an early dose reduction/discontinuation or maintenance treatment strategy: long-term follow-up of a 2-year randomized clinical trial. *JAMA* Psychiatry 70(9): 913–920.

Wykes T, Parr A, Landau S (1999). Group treatment of auditory hallucinations: exploratory study of effectiveness. *Br J Psychiatry* 175: 180–185.

Wykes T, Hayward P, Thomas N, *et al.* (2005). What are the effects of group CBT for voices? A RCT. *Schizophr Res* 77(2–3): 201–210.

Yee L, Korner AJ, McSwiggan S, *et al.* (2005). Persistent hallucinosis in borderline personality disorder. *Compt. Psychiatry* 46: 147–154.

Yoshizumi T, Murase S, Honjo S, *et al.* (2004). Hallucinatory experiences in a community sample of Japanese children. *J Am Acad Child Adolesc Psychiatry* 43(8): 1030–1036.

Young HF, Bentall RB, Slade PD, *et al.* (1987). The role of brief instructions and suggestibility in the elicitation of auditory and visual hallucinations in normal and psychiatric subjects. *J Nerv Ment Dis* 175: 41–48.

Zammit S, Odd D, Holwood J, *et al.* (2009). Investigation whether adverse prenatal and perinatal events are associated with non-clinical symptoms and adult schizophreniform disorder: a 15-year longitudinal study. *Arch Gen Psychiatry* 57: 1053–1058.

Zheng Li, Arthur D (2005). Family education for people with schizophrenia in Beijing, China. *Br J Psychiatry* 187: 339–345.

Zwaard Van der R, Polak MA (1999). Pseudohallucinaties: Een literatuuronderzoek naar de waarde van het concept en de relaties met aanverwante symptomatologie. (Pseudohallucinations: a literature study of concept value and relations with related symptomatology). *Tijdschrift Psychiatrie* 41(1): 25–37.

Index